D1567384

Building
a Web Site
with Ajax

Visual QuickProject Guide

by Larry Ullman

Peachpit Press

Visual QuickProject Guide
Building a Web Site with Ajax
Larry Ullman

Peachpit Press
1249 Eighth Street
Berkeley, CA 94710
510/524-2178
510/524-2221 (fax)

Find us on the Web at: www.peachpit.com
To report errors, please send a note to: errata@peachpit.com
Peachpit Press is a division of Pearson Education.

Copyright © 2008 by Larry Ullman

Editor: Rebecca Gulick
Copy Editor: Liz Welch
Production Editors: Lisa Brazieal and Tracey Croom
Compositor: Roberta Great
Indexers: Ron Strauss and Ann Rogers
Technical Reviewer: Arpad Ray
Cover photo: Quigley Photography/iStockphoto.com

ISBN-13: 978-0-321-52441-6
ISBN-10:   0-321-52441-1

9 8 7 6 5 4 3 2 1

Printed and bound in the United States of America

To Zoe Isabella and Sam Atticus

Special Thanks to...

Rebecca Gulick, the best editor in the land, without whom this book would not exist.

Everyone else at Peachpit Press who help make a "book" an actual book: Lisa Brazieal, Tracey Croom, Roberta Great, Liz Welch, Glenn Bisignani, Ron Strauss, and Ann Rogers.

Arpad Ray, who performed a top-notch technical review.

Jessica, for everything and everything and everything.

Nicole, for helping with the kids so I could actually get some work done (even if I didn't want to).

contents

contents

introduction

The Visual QuickProject Guide you hold in your hands offers a unique way to learn about new technologies. Instead of drowning you in theoretical possbilities and lengthy explanations, this Visual QuickProject Guide uses big illustrations coupled with clear, concise step-by-step instructions to show you how to complete a specific project in a matter of hours.

This particular book in the Visual QuickProject series teaches you how to "roll your own" **Ajax-enabled application**. The specific example will involve managing employees in a company, organized by departments into a type of address book. But the actual example is secondary to the technologies and ideas being taught. By the end of this book, **you'll have a nice, working example; tons of usable code; and an education in Ajax** that you can apply to your own projects.

how Ajax works

Normally, when a client—the user and their Web browser—requests a Web page, the server handles the request, sending the data back to the client. The client loads the data, redrawing the browser with

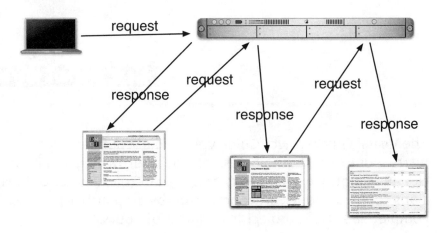

the requested page. For each request, this process is repeated.

Ajax is one way to create **Rich Internet Applications** (RIAs): Web sites that behave more like desktop applications. With an Ajax-enabled application, after the initial loading of the page, **subsequent requests can be handled behind the scenes**. Then the Web browser can be updated without the user

being aware of the server requests, the downloading of data, and so on. In short, Ajax provides a nicer experience for the end user.

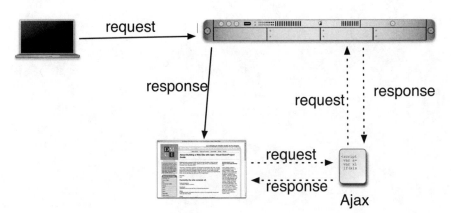

introduction

what you'll learn

Ajax isn't really a "thing" in its own right so much as the combination of many technologies. In this book, those are **(X)HTML**, **CSS**, **JavaScript**, **XML**, **PHP**, **MySQL**, and **SQL**. The heart of an Ajax application is JavaScript and, in particular, a little thing called an **XMLHttpRequest** object. The **XMLHttpRequest** object wraps up all the functionality required to circumvent the old-fashioned client-server process.

However, this book won't teach you how to create just an Ajax-enabled application. You'll see how to create a Web site that also works for those users who can't take advantage of Ajax (because their browser doesn't support JavaScript and **XMLHttpRequest**). Creating an Ajax-enabled application that will still function for non-Ajax-enabled browsers is a two-step process.

In one chapter, you'll create a non-Ajax version of some feature. The non-Ajax version will work for any user and show you, the developer, what this part of the site should do.

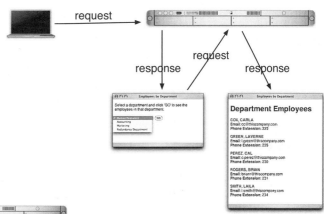

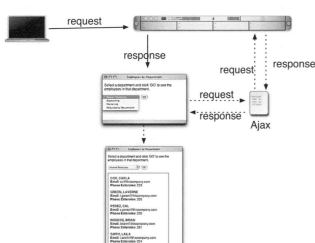

The second step is to add the Ajax layer on top of the non-Ajax version. The intent of the Ajax layer will be the same as the non-Ajax layer, but all the steps will take place in a more sophisticated way for the end user.

how this book works

The **title** of each section explains what idea is covered on that page.

Code blocks show what should be put in the various HTML, CSS, JavaScript, and PHP files. **Sometimes code will appear in boldface to indicate that it is being added to existing code.**

Captions explain what you're doing and why.

Numbered steps indicate the order in which some things must occur.

Screenshots show how the code looks or what it does upon execution.

An **ellipsis (...)** in a code block indicates that there is more code than is being shown. Normally the omitted code has been generated on the previous pages.

Important pieces of code, such as variables, functions, and commands, as well as concepts, are **emphasized**.

---

print the employees

The PHP page prints the list of employees in the given department. To do so, a database query is required. (See **extra bits** on page 41.)

```
...
if ($did > 0) {
    require_once('mysql.inc.php');
    $q = "SELECT * FROM employees WHERE department_id=$did
ORDER BY last_name, rst_name";
    $r = mysql_query($q, $dbc);
    if (mysql_num_rows($r) > 0) {
```

1 **Include the database connection script** (written in the previous chapter).

2 **Query the database**, looking for employees in the given department.

```
    while ($row = mysql_fetch_array($r, MYSQL_ASSOC)) {
        echo "<p><span class=\"name\">{$row['last_name']},
{$row[' rst_name']}</span><br />
        <strong>Email</strong>: {$row['email']}<br />
        <strong>Phone Extension</strong>: {$row['phone_ext']}
        </p>\n";
    } // End of WHILE loop.
```

3 **Fetch any returned records and print them** with a little bit of HTML and CSS formatting.

browsing using Ajax   33

The **extra bits** section at the end of each chapter contains tips and tricks that you might like to know. The **heading** for each group of tips matches the section title. The **page number** next to the heading makes it easy to find the section to which the tips belong.

extra bits (cont.)

prepare the form data p. 65

- When a form is submitted using the GET method, you'll see the form data in the URL, with a syntax of `page.php?this_item=this_value&that_item=that_value`. This is the same syntax used by POST, but the data isn't sent in the URL and you don't need the question mark.

- All of the form data needs to be run through the `encodeURIComponent()` function to make it safe to send to the PHP page. Rather than apply that function to each value separately, using a **for** loop on an array of form elements lets us accomplish the same thing with less code.

- The **plus sign in JavaScript** is used to perform **concatenation**: appending one string onto another. In PHP, the period does the same thing.

- If you wanted to send XML data to the PHP script, you would set the **Content-Type** to **text/xml**.

complete the function p. 66

- When using the GET method, use the value null as the only argument when calling **send()**. Any data sent over GET is appended to the URL itself. When using POST, you need to provide the data when you call **send()**, as it's not sent in the URL.

prepare for XML p. 67

- The PHP script sends its response as XML data, not as a normal Web page. Everything PHP will print will be part of this XML.

- The XML data being created is really like the data in an HTML page, where there's one root element and any number of nested subelements. For this example, the root element will be called **response** and there will be two subelements. There can be zero or more elements called **error** and there will always be exactly one element called **result**. In comparison, an HTML page has a root element called **html**, two subelements named **head** and **body**, and more subelements within those.

adding records via Ajax   83

required tools

This book covers the basics of Ajax but not of Web development. The assumption is that you already have, and know how to use, certain tools and technologies.

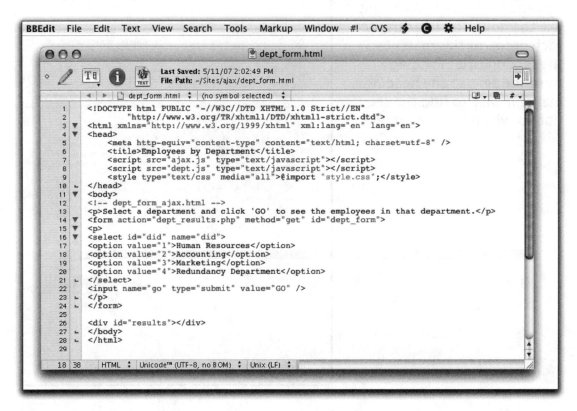

A **text editor, integrated development environment** (IDE), or **What You See Is What You Get** (WYSIWYG) editor is a must. This might be BBEdit on the Macintosh (my personal favorite text editor), Notepad on Windows, Eclipse (a popular, open source IDE), or Dreamweaver (a popular, commercial WYSIWYG app). It doesn't matter what you use as long as it's something in which you can create and edit plain-text files.

The second requirement is a **Web browser**, but if you have a computer, you have one of these. Because Ajax can have browser-specific issues, you'll want to have **many different browsers** on many different operating systems, if at all possible. I tested the book's examples using Internet Explorer and Firefox on Windows (XP) and using Safari, Firefox, and Opera on Mac OS X.

I **highly recommend that you use Firefox** for development and initial testing purposes, as it's far less quirky than Internet Explorer and has many great debugging tools.

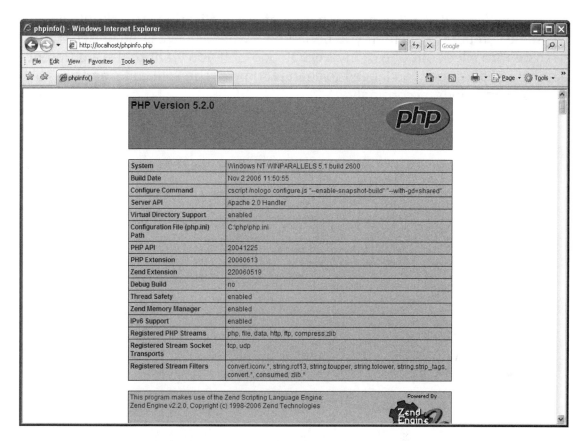

The most advanced requirement is a **PHP-enabled Web server**. You'll need to run PHP through Apache, Microsoft's Internet Information Server, or some other Web server. This can be on your own computer or on a hosted server. If you don't know what PHP is, you should probably check out one of my PHP books before cracking this one (see "the next step" for recommendations).

required tools (cont.)

If you're using a hosted server, you'll need to have an **FTP** (File Transfer Protocol) application or similar option for uploading files to the server from your computer.

Finally, you'll need **MySQL** or another database application. This should be on the same computer as PHP. If you don't know what MySQL is, again see "the next step" to check out one of my MySQL books. If you want to use a different database application, you'll need to change some of the PHP code, and possibly the SQL commands, accordingly.

companion web site

The companion Web site for this book can be found at
www.DMCInsights.com/ajax/.

Head to the **downloads** area to get all of the book's code so you don't have to type it yourself.

After reading the book, check out the **extras** section for more information, alternative versions of the examples, and more.

If you have questions or need any assistance, head to the **forum.**

the next step

The focus in this book is creating a very good and usable Ajax-enabled application. There are a lot of technologies involved, the most important of which is JavaScript.

For more discussion of PHP, MySQL, SQL, and XML, see some of my other books. A basic introduction to PHP can be found in my **PHP for the World Wide Web, 2nd Edition: Visual QuickStart Guide** (ISBN 0-321-24565-2). I provide thorough coverage of SQL and MySQL in **MySQL, Second Edition: Visual QuickStart Guide** (ISBN 0-321-37573-4). All of this information, and much more, is put together in my **PHP and MySQL for Dynamic Web Sites, Second Edition: Visual QuickPro Guide** (ISBN 0-321-33657-7). And I discuss XML in one chapter of my **PHP 5 Advanced: Visual QuickPro Guide** (ISBN 0-321-37601-3).

For more information on (X)HTML and CSS, see Elizabeth Castro's excellent **HTML, XHTML, and CSS, Sixth Edition: Visual QuickStart Guide** (ISBN 0-321-43084-0).

1. creating the database

The Ajax-enabled Web site we'll be creating in this book uses a **database on the server** to store all of the content: a list of employees, along with some pertinent sample information about them. To begin, we need to create and populate this database. For the example, I'll be using **MySQL**, a popular open-source database application.

This chapter covers what you need to know to create the database but assumes that you have access to a MySQL installation. I'll demonstrate the steps in this chapter using two different interfaces: **the command-line mysql client** and the **Web-based phpMyAdmin**. If you have any questions or problems with this chapter's instructions, see my book **MySQL, Second Edition: Visual QuickStart Guide** (ISBN 0-321-37573-4) or search the Web.

access MySQL

If you're running MySQL on your own computer, or have command-line access to your server, **log into the mysql client**. You'll need to **enter a username and password combination.** These values must already be established in MySQL in order to work. (See **extra bits** on page 9.)

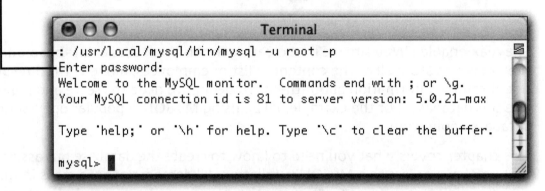

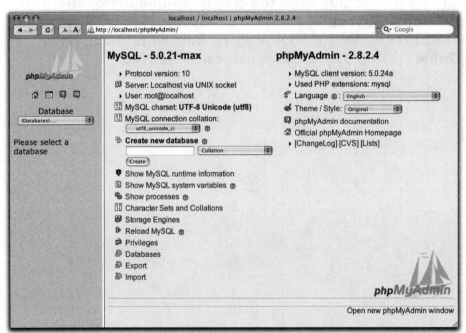

If you're running MySQL on a remote server, or you just prefer not to go command-line, **use phpMyAdmin in a Web browser**. It must already be preconfigured to access MySQL.

creating the database

make the database

1 On the command line, using the **mysql client**, type **CREATE DATABASE ajax**, followed by a **semicolon (;)**, and press Enter or Return. If you've accessed MySQL as a user with permission to create databases, you'll see a message saying that the query was OK and that one row was affected.

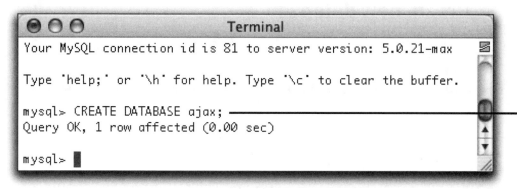

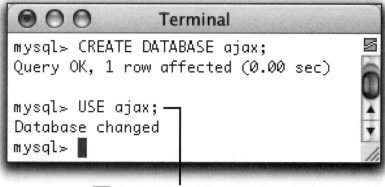

2 Type **USE ajax**, followed by a **semicolon**, and press Enter or Return.

make the database (cont.)

1 If you are using **phpMyAdmin**, type the name of the database—I'm using the name **ajax**—in the **Create new database** box, and then click **Create**. (You can ignore the Collation menu; see **extra bits** on page 9.)

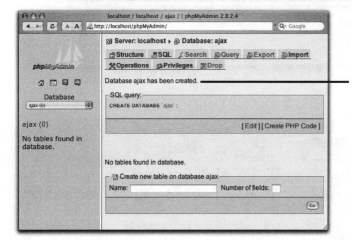

The resulting page should show that the database was created.

2 If phpMyAdmin did not automatically select the new database for you, use the drop-down menu on the left to select it. (phpMyAdmin will likely have already selected that database for you.)

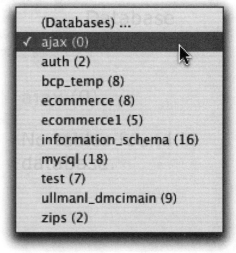

creating the database

make the tables

If you are using the command-line mysql client, create the tables in the database by running two **CREATE TABLE** commands. (See **extra bits** on page 10.)

```
● ● ●                           Terminal
mysql> CREATE TABLE departments (
    ->     department_id TINYINT UNSIGNED NOT NULL AUTO_INCREMENT PRIMARY KEY,
    ->     department VARCHAR(30) NOT NULL,
    ->     UNIQUE (department)
    -> );
Query OK, 0 rows affected (0.08 sec)

mysql> CREATE TABLE employees (
    ->     employee_id INT UNSIGNED NOT NULL AUTO_INCREMENT PRIMARY KEY,
    ->     department_id TINYINT UNSIGNED NOT NULL,
    ->     first_name VARCHAR(20) NOT NULL,
    ->     last_name VARCHAR(40) NOT NULL,
    ->     email VARCHAR(60) NOT NULL,
    ->     phone_ext SMALLINT UNSIGNED NOT NULL,
    ->     INDEX (department_id),
    ->     INDEX (last_name),
    ->     UNIQUE (email)
    -> );
Query OK, 0 rows affected (0.00 sec)

mysql> █
```

```
CREATE TABLE departments (
  department_id TINYINT UNSIGNED NOT NULL AUTO_INCREMENT
PRIMARY KEY,
  department VARCHAR(30) NOT NULL,
  UNIQUE (department)
);
```

```
CREATE TABLE employees (
  employee_id INT UNSIGNED NOT NULL AUTO_INCREMENT
PRIMARY KEY,
  department_id TINYINT UNSIGNED NOT NULL,
  first_name VARCHAR(20) NOT NULL,
  last_name VARCHAR(40) NOT NULL,
  email VARCHAR(60) NOT NULL,
  phone_ext SMALLINT UNSIGNED NOT NULL,
  INDEX (department_id),
  INDEX (last_name),
  UNIQUE (email)
);
```

make the tables (cont.)

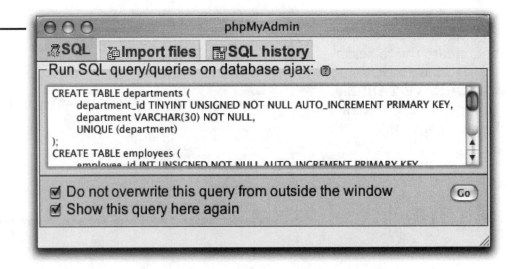

If you are using **phpMyAdmin**, you can run your commands in the **SQL pop-up window** or through the **SQL tab**.

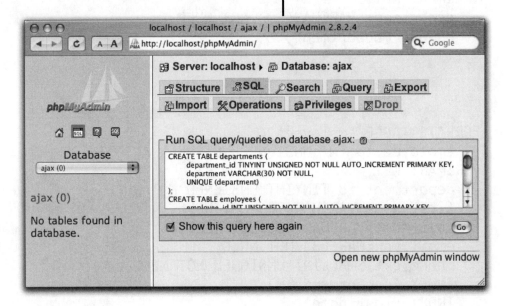

creating the database

populate the tables

Finally, populate the tables in the database by running these two **INSERT** commands in the mysql client, if you're using it. (See **extra bits** on page 10.)

```
INSERT INTO departments (department) VALUES
('Human Resources'),
('Accounting'),
('Marketing'),
('Redundancy Department');
```

```
INSERT INTO employees (department_id, first_name,
last_name, email, phone_ext) VALUES
(1, 'Laila', 'Smith', 'l.smith@thiscompany.com', 234),
(1, 'Laverne', 'Green', 'l.green@thiscompany.com', 235),
(1, 'Cal', 'Perez', 'c.perez@thiscompany.com', 230),
(1, 'Brian', 'Rogers', 'brianr@thiscompany.com', 231),
(1, 'Carla', 'Cox', 'cc@thiscompany.com', 233),
(2, 'Ezra', 'Howard', 'e.howard@thiscompany.com', 122),
(2, 'Gideon', 'Gray', 'g.gray@thiscompany.com', 128),
```

```
continued
   (2, 'Penelope', 'Brooks', 'pb@thiscompany.com', 129),
   (2, 'Olive', 'Kelly', 'olive@thiscompany.com', 120),
   (2, 'Justine', 'Sanders', 'j.sanders@thiscompany.com',
       123),
   (2, 'Zoe', 'Ford', 'zoe@thiscompany.com', 125),
   (3, 'Sam', 'Fisher', 'sam@thiscompany.com', 385),
   (3, 'Henry', 'Barnes', 'henry@thiscompany.com', 386),
   (3, 'Eleanor', 'Wood', 'eleanor@thiscompany.com', 387),
   (4, 'Emmet', 'Humphries', 'e.humphries@thiscompany.
       com', 401),
   (4, 'Conrad', 'Madsen', 'conrad@thiscompany.com', 410),
   (4, 'Maude', 'Ernst', 'm.ernst@thiscompany.com', 409),
   (4, 'Stella', 'Redding', 's.redding@thiscompany.com',
       408),
   (4, 'Nat', 'Fugate', 'nat@thiscompany.com', 407),
   (4, 'Hazel', 'Hay', 'h.hay@thiscompany.com', 402);
```

If using **phpMyAdmin**, you can run your commands in the
SQL pop-up window or through the SQL tab.

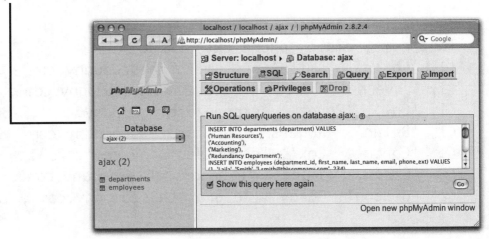

extra bits

access MySQL p. 2

- You can use pretty much any database application for your Web sites, not just MySQL. If there's one you're more comfortable with, feel free to switch. (Note that you would also need to change the PHP code in the rest of the book.)

- The mysql client can be tricky if you're not used to it. If you have any problems, check out the MySQL manual, a book on MySQL, or this book's support site at **www.dmcinsights.com/ajax/**. Many people find phpMyAdmin, also used in this chapter, to be an easier option.

make the database p. 4

- If you're using MySQL on a hosted Web site, your host will likely provide you with phpMyAdmin access. They may or may not let you create databases, though. If not, just use the database you have already (assuming it does not have tables called **departments** and **employees**).

- A database's **collation** refers to the types of language characters the database will support. If you don't specify a collation, the MySQL default collation will be used. This is normally fine.

extra bits (cont.)

make the tables p. 5

- Both tables are defined in a minimalist way. You can add columns if you'd like, but you'll need to change the **INSERT** commands (later in the chapter) accordingly.

- The SQL commands in this chapter, and all of the book's code, can be downloaded from **www.dmcinsights.com/ajax/**.

- The **departments** table has a unique index on the **department** column, ensuring that each department is listed only once.

- There is a one-to-many relationship between the two tables. Each employee can be in only one department but each department can have many employees. This relationship is represented by the **department_id** column, which is in both tables.

- You can create tables in phpMyAdmin using either of the SQL text areas as shown in the examples or by using the create table prompt. To use the prompt, provide phpMyAdmin with the name of the table and the number of fields, and it will create a form where you can enter all of the column definitions.

populate the tables p. 7

- The data being inserted isn't important, so long as you populate the tables with some information. You can make up your own records or download the SQL commands from the book's corresponding Web site at **www.dmcinsights.com/ajax/**.

- The **department_id** value for each employee must correspond to an actual **department_id** from the **departments** table.

creating the database

2. **browsing employees**

This book's example contains three facets: browsing employees by department, adding employees, and searching for employees by last name. For each section, we'll create a non-Ajax version, and then apply the Ajax elements on top. In this chapter, we'll make a non-Ajax way to browse employees. To do so, we'll create **one HTML page**, **two PHP scripts**, and a **CSS style sheet**.

The non-Ajax pages can act as a model for how the Ajax layer should behave, and more importantly, if anyone accessing this site cannot use the Ajax-enabled pages, the site will still be fully functional for them. Also, two of the files generated in this chapter—one PHP script and the CSS document—will be used by all of this book's examples, Ajax and non-Ajax alike.

You may find it easiest to follow along by first downloading all the code from the book's corresponding Web site (**www.dmcinsights.com/ajax/**).

what we'll do

1 First, on pages 13-14, we'll create a **simple HTML form**.

The HTML form will have a **drop-down menu listing the departments**. These values will match those inserted into the database in Chapter 1, "creating the database."

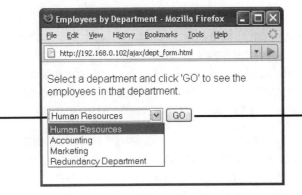

When the user clicks **GO**, the form will be submitted to a PHP script.

2 On pages 15-17, the **PHP script** that handles the HTML form will be written.

The **script shows the employees** for the department selected in the HTML form. These employees come from the database created in Chapter 1.

3 Because the PHP page's results come from a database, **a special PHP script** will be written on pages 18 solely for the purpose of **connecting to the database**.

Department Employees

BARNES, HENRY
Email: henry@thiscompany.com
Phone Extension: 386

FISHER, SAM
Email: sam@thiscompany.com
Phone Extension: 385

WOOD, ELEANOR
Email: eleanor@thiscompany.com
Phone Extension: 387

4 On pages 19-20, a very simple **style sheet** will be made and added to the HTML page, giving the Web pages a slightly (but only slightly) more attractive appearance.

5 As a last step, we'll **test** what we've built to make sure it all works.

At the end of this chapter, in the **extra bits** section, you'll find more information, tips, and recommendations regarding all of these steps.

browsing employees

create an HTML page

The very first step in the Ajax application is a basic HTML form. Use any text editing application to make a new HTML document. (See **extra bits** on page 22.)

```
<!DOCTYPE html PUBLIC "-//W3C//DTD XHTML 1.0 Strict//
EN"
"http://www.w3.org/TR/xhtml1/DTD/xhtml1-strict.dtd">
<html xmlns="http://www.w3.org/1999/xhtml" xml:
lang="en" lang="en">
<head>
   <meta http-equiv="content-type" content="text/html;
charset=utf-8" />
   <title>Employees by Department</title>
</head>
<body>
<!-- dept_form.html -->
</body>
</html>
```

All this jibberish is just the framework of an HTML page. The only bit of text here that will be apparent to the end user is the **<title>** value, which shows up in the top of the user's Web browser (see the figure on page 12).

Save this file as **dept_form.html** and place it in a directory on your Web server.

add the HTML form

Just before the form, **add instructions for the user**.

The value for the form's **action** should be the name of the PHP script that will handle this form. Set the **method** as **get**. Give the form a meaningful **id** value. (See **extra bits** on page 22.)

```
...
<body>
<!-- dept_form.html -->
<p>Select a department and click 'GO' to see the
employees in that department.</p>
<form action="dept_results.php" method="get" id="dept_
    form">
  <p>
    <select id="did" name="did">
    <option value="1">Human Resources</option>
    <option value="2">Accounting</option>
    <option value="3">Marketing</option>
    <option value="4">Redundancy Department</option>
    </select>
    <input name="go" type="submit" value="GO" />
  </p>
</form>
</body>
</html>
```

The form contains a **select menu**, listing the departments. The value of each option is the department number from the database. The **name and id** of this form element must be **did** (short for department ID).

The form needs a **submit button**, too.

14   **browsing employees**

start a PHP page

The main PHP page handles the form submission. It should also be a valid HTML document, so start with those tags. (See **extra bits** on page 22.)

```
<!DOCTYPE html PUBLIC "-//W3C//DTD XHTML 1.0 Strict//
EN"
"http://www.w3.org/TR/xhtml1/DTD/xhtml1-strict.dtd">
<html xmlns="http://www.w3.org/1999/xhtml" xml:
lang="en" lang="en">
<head>
  <meta http-equiv="content-type" content="text/html;
charset=utf-8" />
  <title>Employees by Department</title>
</head>
<body>
<h1>Department Employees</h1>
<?php # dept_results.php
?>
</body>
</html>
```

All of the page's functionality will go in between the PHP tags.

This file must be saved as **dept_results.php** and placed in the same directory as **dept_form.html**.

print the employees

1 Within the PHP tags, start by making sure that a **valid department ID** was received. The department ID must be an **integer greater than 0**. (See **extra bits** on page 23.)

```php
...
<?php # dept_results.php
$did = 0;
if (isset($_GET['did'])) {
   $did = (int) $_GET['did'];
}
if ($did > 0) {
   require_once('mysql.inc.php');
   $q = "SELECT * FROM employees WHERE department_
id=$did ORDER BY last_name, first_name";
   $r = mysql_query($q, $dbc);
   if (mysql_num_rows($r) > 0) {
      while ($row = mysql_fetch_array($r, MYSQL_ASSOC))
{

      echo "<p><span class=\"name\">{$row['last_
name']}, {$row['first_name']}</span><br />
      <strong>Email</strong>: {$row['email']}<br />
      <strong>Phone Extension</strong>: {$row['phone_
ext']}
      </p>\n";
      }
```

2 Then **include the database connection script** (to be written next).

3 **Query the database**, looking for employees in the given department.

4 **Fetch any returned records and print them** with a little bit of HTML and CSS formatting.

report on any errors

The PHP script should let the user know if an error occurred. **Complete the two IF conditionals** created in the previous steps.

```
...
</p>\n";
    }
} else {
    echo '<p class="error">There are no employees
listed for the given department.</p>';
  }
} else {
    echo '<p class="error">Please select a valid
department from the drop-down menu in order to view
its employees.</p>';
}
?>
...
```

1 The first **else** clause will apply if the database query **didn't return any results**.

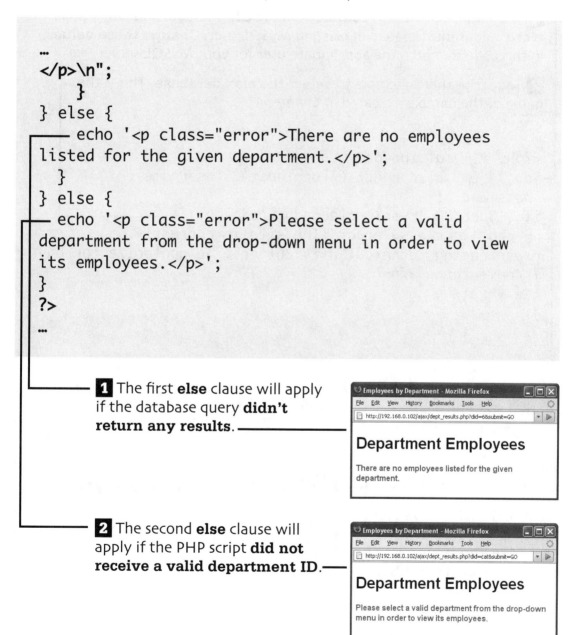

Department Employees

There are no employees listed for the given department.

2 The second **else** clause will apply if the PHP script **did not receive a valid department ID**.

Department Employees

Please select a valid department from the drop-down menu in order to view its employees.

connect to the database

Create a new, blank PHP script that connects to the database. This script does not require the basic HTML tags. (See **extra bits** on page 23.)

1 The script first tries to **connect to MySQL**. The **username** and **password** values must match an existing MySQL user. **Change these values** in this code to match the appropriate user for your MySQL server.

2 The script then attempts to **select the ajax database**. This is the name of the database created in Chapter 1.

```php
<?php # mysql.inc.php
$dbc = @mysql_connect ('localhost', 'username',
'password');
if (!$dbc OR !mysql_select_db ('ajax')) {
  echo '<p class="error">The site is currently
experiencing technical difficulties. We apologize for any
inconvenience.</p>';
   exit();
}
?>
```

3 Error messages are printed if either attempt fails. If so, the script then terminates because there's no need to go on without a database connection.

4 Save this file as **mysql.inc.php** and place it in the same directory on your Web server as **dept_form.html**.

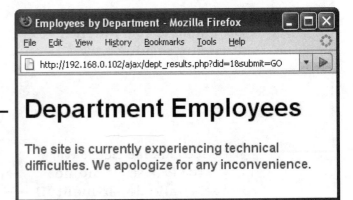

browsing employees

create a style sheet

The CSS style sheet is a separate document that dictates how the pages look. Create a new file in your test editor or IDE, containing this code. (See **extra bits** on page 24.)

```css
body {
    font-family: sans-serif;
}
.name {
    font-weight: bold;
    text-transform: uppercase;
    color: #009;
}
.error {
    font-weight: bold;
    color: #C00
}
#results {
    border: medium solid #390;
    display: none;
    padding-left: 10px;
    width: 300px;
}
```

The **body** section sets the default font for the entire HTML page.

The second section formats text with a **class value of name**. That would be the employee's name in the listing of results in **dept_results.php**.

The third section applies some formatting to **any errors** (which will have a **class value of error**), like those created in both PHP scripts.

The final section applies to any block with an **id value of results**. You'll use this when adding the Ajax layer in the next chapter.

Save this file as **style.css** and place it in the same directory on your Web server as every other file.

use the style sheet

For the style sheet to be used, it must be referenced in the HTML and PHP pages. Do so by adding a line to the **<head>** section of both files:

```
...
<title>Employees by Department</title>
  <style type="text/css" media="all">@import "style.
css";</style>
</head>
<body>
...
```

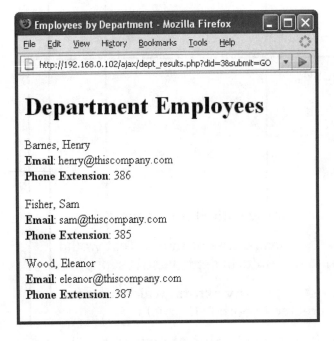

The style sheet is mostly cosmetic. The non-Ajax layer will work perfectly fine without it, but it won't look as nice.

test the pages

1 **Load the HTML page** in your Web browser to test what we've created so far.

The address **must begin with http://** for this to work. (See **extra bits** on page 24.)

2 Select a department and click **GO**.

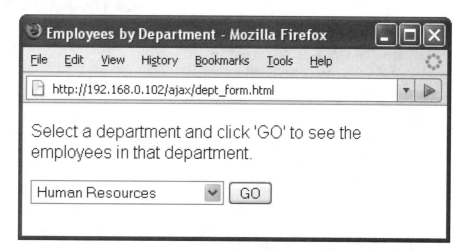

3 The PHP page should show the results.

extra bits

create an HTML page p. 13

- HTML, JavaScript, CSS, and PHP can be written in nearly any application. I prefer to use a simple text editor (specifically, BBEdit on Mac OS X), but use what you like. People who focus on Web development often like a WYSIWYG (What You See Is What You Get) tool like Dreamweaver. PHP developers sometimes lean toward IDEs (integrated development enviroments) like Eclipse, NuSphere's PhpED, or Zend Studio.

- For the HTML in this book, I'll be using the **XHTML 1.0 Strict** standard. For more information on this, see a dedicated HTML resource, like Elizabeth Castro's most excellent HTML, XHTML, & CSS: Visual QuickStart Guide, Sixth Edition (ISBN-13: 978-0321430847).

- Both the Ajax and non-Ajax versions of this example use PHP, which means that **you must have a PHP-enabled Web server** to test the examples on. This can be your own computer, if you've installed PHP, or a remotely hosted Web site, if you have one of those.

- For the sake of simplicity, every file created in this book will just go in the same folder on the server.

add the HTML form p. 14

- When it comes to handling HTML forms, the **action** and the **method** are the two most important considerations. The **action** tells the browser to what page the form data should be sent. The **method** tells the browser how that data should be sent. The **get** method sends the data in the URL.

- Normally I would have PHP dynamically generate any drop-down menu that corresponds to a database table. I'm saving steps by not doing so here.

start a PHP page p. 15

- PHP is a server-side language used to dynamically generate HTML code (among other purposes). Anything within the PHP tags—**<?php** and **?>**—will be treated as PHP code. Anything outside of those tags will immediately be sent to the Web browser and treated as HTML.

print the employees p. 16

- When it comes time to test this part of the Web site, if you have problems with this page you'll need to employ some standard PHP-database debugging techniques. Begin by printing out the query being run (add **echo $q;** after the query is created). Then run the query using another interface, like the command-line **mysql client** or the Web-based **phpMyAdmin**. These two steps will confirm what the query's results are.

- Another useful debugging technique for any PHP script is to view the dynamically-generated HTML source code in your Web browser. Sometimes the problem can be hidden there.

- For more information on PHP and PHP-MySQL interactions, see my book **PHP and MySQL for Dynamic Web Sites: Visual QuickPro Guide, Second Edition** (ISBN-13: 978-0321336576) or search the Web.

connect to the database p. 18

- As many PHP scripts in this application will use the database, it's best to create one script that establishes that connection. Every page that requires a database connection will then include this file.

- The **mysql.inc.php** script can be a likely cause of problems. To guarantee that it works when it comes time to test the site, make sure you are using a **username and password combination** that has access to the **ajax** database. If you have any problems, check out the MySQL manual, a book on MySQL (like my **MySQL, Second Edition: Visual QuickStart Guide** (ISBN-13: 978-0321375735), or this book's support Web site at www.dmcinsights.com/ajax/.

create a style sheet p. 19

- I'm making only minimal use of CSS (Cascading Style Sheets) in this book, but CSS is definitely part of Rich Internet Applications (RIA), like the one being created. For more information on this subject, search the Web or check out Elizabeth Castro's HTML, XHTML, & CSS: Visual QuickStart Guide, Sixth Edition (ISBN-13: 978-0321430847).

- The most interesting of the style definitions is the one for items with an **id value of results**. Such items will not be displayed when the page is first loaded. Then, when appropriate, the JavaScript will fill that section with results and make it visible. This all takes place in the Ajax layer, created in the next chapter.

test the pages p. 21

- All PHP pages must be run through a URL in order to work. Therefore, the HTML form must also be run through a URL (the address must begin with `http://`). If the address begins with `file://`, the PHP script handling the form won't do its thing.

- Getting these components to work is a perfect first step in creating an Ajax-enabled layer. It's easier to debug these pages than it will be once JavaScript and other technologies are added to the mix.

- Debugging PHP may be the hardest skill for the beginner to learn—unfortunately, the beginner will end up doing the most debugging (it's a "trial by fire" situation). If you have problems getting these pages to work, see the book's Web site at **www.dmcinsights.com/ajax/**, for assistance.

3. browsing using Ajax

In the previous chapter, we created the non-Ajax parts of the employee browsing pages. Although the focus in this book is on Ajax, it's very important to have working, non-Ajax components in place for those who can't take advantage of the lovely Ajax interface. In this chapter we'll place the Ajax layer on top of the existing one.

The Ajax components consist of three files: **one JavaScript file** that will provide **all-purpose, browser-safe Ajax functionality; another JavaScript** file that will provide **page-specific functionality**; and **one PHP script** that will handle the **server-side needs** of the Ajax layer. To make these additions active, the main **HTML form** will be **slightly modified** as a last step.

what we'll do

1 First, on pages 27-28, we'll create a **JavaScript file** that makes a browser-specific supported Ajax object. That object will be used by any page requiring Ajax functionality.

2 On pages 29-31, a **second JavaScript file** that defines the functionality specific to the employee-browsing aspect of the example will be started.

3 A **new PHP script** will be written on pages 32-34. This script will return the results of the Ajax request to the JavaScript.

4 On pages 35 and 36, the **second JavaScript page will be completed**, handling the PHP request and updating the HTML page.

5 Next, the **HTML page will be modified** to include the Ajax layer on page 37.

6 As a last step, on page 38 we'll **test** what we've built to make sure it all works.

At the end of this chapter, in the **extra bits** section, you'll find more information, tips, and recommendations regarding all of these steps.

make a function

One JavaScript file will contain all of the code for establishing generic Ajax functionality. Use any text editing application to make a new JavaScript document. (See **extra bits** on page 39.)

```
function getXMLHttpRequestObject() {
  var ajax = false;
}
```

1 The JavaScript function is called **getXMLHttpRequestObject()** (it's a long but descriptive name). This function creates a browser-specific XMLHttpRequest object, stored in the variable **ajax**.

2 The function assumes no Ajax support to start (the **ajax** variable is initialized with the Boolean value of **false**). In the rest of the function, browsers have to "prove" they can take advantage of the Ajax functionality.

check for Ajax support

Within the function, check what kind of **XMLHttpRequest object** the browser supports. If a browser supports a specific type of **XMLHttpRequest** object, make the **ajax** variable an object of that type. (See **extra bits** on page 39.)

1 Most Web browsers—Apple's Safari 1.2 and later, Mozilla and Firefox, Opera 8 and later, and newer versions of Internet Explorer—should meet this first condition.

```
function getXMLHttpRequestObject() {
  var ajax = false;
  if (window.XMLHttpRequest) {
    ajax = new XMLHttpRequest();
  } else if (window.ActiveXObject) {
    try {
      ajax = new ActiveXObject("Msxml2.XMLHTTP");
    } catch (e) {
      try {
        ajax = new ActiveXObject("Microsoft.XMLHTTP");
      } catch (e) { }
    }
  }
  return ajax;
}
```

2 Older versions of Internet Explorer (that have ActiveX enabled) should get an **XMLHttpRequest** object from one of these two lines.

3 Finally, this function returns the **ajax** variable.

4 Save this file as **ajax.js** and place it in the same directory on your Web server as every other file.

call the function

The **ajax.js** file defines a function that creates an **XMLHttpRequest** object, but it doesn't actually use that object. Another JavaScript file will do that for each specific instance, like the HTML form already created. Use any text editing application to make a new JavaScript document. (See **extra bits** on page 40.)

1 The first line tells the Web browsers to run the **init()** function after loading the entire page. The **init()** function sets up all the Ajax activity.

```
window.onload = init;
function init() {
    var ajax = getXMLHttpRequestObject();
    if (ajax) {
    } // End of ajax IF.
} // End of init() function.
```

2 The **init()** function calls the **getXMLHttpRequestObject()** function to get a valid, browser-specific object.

3 The **init()** function then checks to see if the **ajax** variable has a valid value. With supported browsers, **ajax** will be an **XMLHttpRequest** object. With nonsupported browsers, **ajax** will have a value of **false**, and this conditional will be false.

set up the Ajax

Now the JavaScript should tell the browser what actions should be taken when certain events occur. (See **extra bits** on page 40.)

1 The **init()** function next checks to see if the browser supports the **Document Object Model (DOM)** and, specifically, if the page has an element with an **id** of **results**.

```
...
    if (ajax) {
        if (document.getElementById('results')) {
            document.getElementById('dept_form').onsubmit =
function() {
                var did = document.getElementById('did').
value;
```

2 If the browser supports it, an **onsubmit()** event is attached to the form (which has an **id** value of **dept_form**). In other words, when the form is submitted, do the following...

browsing using Ajax

3 Provide to the **ajax** object the name of the page that should be sent the request. This is **dept_results_ajax.php**, to be written next. The request will be made using the **get** method. ─────────────────

4 As part of that request, the department ID value (from the form) will be passed along in the URL.

```
        ajax.open('get', 'dept_results_ajax.php?did='
+ encodeURIComponent(did));
            ajax.onreadystatechange = function() {
            handleResponse(ajax);
        }
```

5 When the **ajax** object's **readyState** value changes, the **handleResponse()** function should be called, passing that function this same **ajax** object.

6 Then the actual Ajax request is made.

```
        ajax.send(null);
        return false;
        } // End of anonymous function.
    } // End of DOM check.
  } // End of ajax IF.
...
```

7 Finally, the function returns a value of **false** to tell the Web browser not to actually submit the form (since the Ajax is handling the form submission).

8 Save this file as **dept.js** and place it in the same directory on your Web server as every other file.

begin the PHP page

A new PHP script will handle the Ajax request. It works exactly like **dept_results.php** (which we created in the previous chapter) except that it doesn't need to print the opening and closing HTML tags. Use any text editing application to make a new PHP document.

1 The page starts by making sure that it receives a valid department ID in the URL. For security purposes, assume we don't have a valid department ID.

2 If a department ID was passed to this page in the URL, **type-cast** it (force it to be an integer).

```php
<?php # dept_results_ajax.php
$did = 0;
if (isset($_GET['did'])) {
    $did = (int) $_GET['did'];
}
if ($did > 0) {
} else { // Invalid department ID!
    echo '<p class="error">Please select a valid department
from the drop-down menu in order to view its employees.</
p>';
}
?>
```

3 If the result is a positive integer, we can go ahead and query the database.

4 If the result isn't a positive integer, print an error message instead.

print the employees

The PHP page prints the list of employees in the given department. To do so, a database query is required. (See **extra bits** on page 41.)

```
...
if ($did > 0) {
    require_once('mysql.inc.php');
    $q = "SELECT * FROM employees WHERE department_
id=$did ORDER BY last_name, first_name";
    $r = mysql_query($q, $dbc);
```

1 **Include the database connection script** (written in the previous chapter).

2 **Query the database**, looking for employees in the given department.

```
    while ($row = mysql_fetch_array($r, MYSQL_ASSOC)) {
        echo "<p><span class=\"name\">{$row['last_name']},
{$row['first_name']}</span><br />
        <strong>Email</strong>: {$row['email']}<br />
        <strong>Phone Extension</strong>: {$row['phone_ext']}
        </p>\n";
    } // End of WHILE loop.
```

3 **Fetch any returned records and print them** with a little bit of HTML and CSS formatting.

print the employees (cont.)

4 Print an error if no employees were found in the given department.

```
  } else { // No employees.
    echo '<p class="error">There are no employees listed
for the given department.</p>';
  }
mysql_close($dbc);
} else { // Invalid department ID!
...
```

5 Close the database connection.

6 Save this file as **dept_results_ajax.php** and place it in the same directory on your Web server as every other file.

handle the response

The PHP page prints out the employees, but since Ajax is being used, this printout will actually be returned to the original JavaScript. Add this new function to the **dept.js** JavaScript file. (See **extra bits** on page 41.)

1 This JavaScript function is called when the **ajax** object's **readyState** value changes (see the **init()** function). The function receives the Ajax object when called.

2 The function shouldn't do anything until **readyState** has a value of 4, meaning that the Ajax transaction is complete.

```
function handleResponse(ajax) {
    if (ajax.readyState == 4) {
        if ((ajax.status == 200) || (ajax.status == 304) )
{
        } else {
            document.getElementById('dept_form').submit();
        }
    }
}
```

3 If the **status code** is equal to either 200 or 304, the returned results should be fine to use.

4 If we didn't get a valid status code back from the Ajax request, we should formally submit the form to the handling PHP page (as if the Ajax layer didn't exist at all).

display the results

The final step in the Ajax process is to display the results by putting what the PHP page returned on the HTML page. This code completes the **handleResponse()** function. (See **extra bits** on page 41.)

1 The **results** variable now refers to a specific area in the DOM of the HTML page.

```
...
if ((ajax.status == 200) || (ajax.status == 304) ) {
   var results = document.getElementById('results');
   results.innerHTML = ajax.responseText;
   results.style.display = 'block';
} else {
...
```

2 The text in the **results** area is set to the returned response from the Ajax request. In this case, that's whatever the PHP page printed out.

3 The **results** area of the HTML page is not initially displayed, so it needs to have its **display** style changed.

modify the HTML

The final step is to modify the HTML form page so that the JavaScript will work.

```
...
    <title>Employees by Department</title>
    <script src="ajax.js" type="text/javascript"></
script>
    <script src="dept.js" type="text/javascript"></
script>
    <style type="text/css" media="all">@import "style.
css";</style>
</form>
...
```

1 Include the two JavaScript pages in this page.

```
...
</form>
<div id="results"></div>
</body>
</html>
```

2 Create a **div** section with an **id** of **results**. The results returned by the Ajax request will go here.

test the Ajax layer

Now that all of the work is done, it's time to see how things
turned out. (See **extra bits** on page 42.)

1 **Load the HTML** ——
page in your Web
browser.

The address **must
begin with http://**
for this to work.

2 Select a depart-
ment and click GO. ——

3 The HTML page ——
should show the
results without
going to a new
page or reloading
this page.

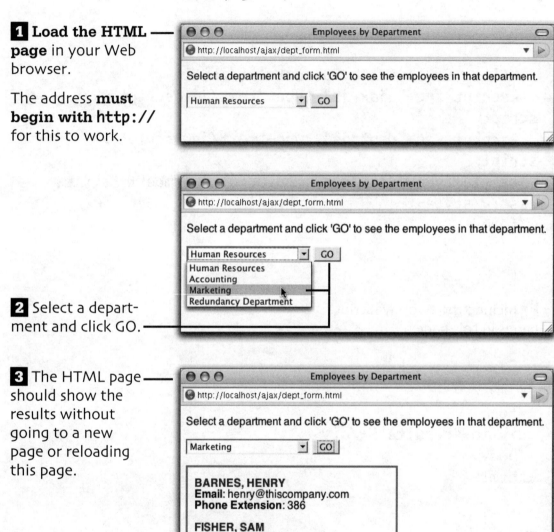

extra bits

make a function p. 27

- JavaScript, like most languages, allows you to define your own functions. Start with the word **function**, followed by the name of the function, followed by parentheses. The function's body goes between curly braces. The function's name can contain only letters, numbers, and the underscore. It cannot begin with a number, and it also can't be the same as an existing keyword in JavaScript.

- Variables declared in a function using the keyword **var** are **local** to that function. This is to say, the variables only exist within that function.

- If a function takes **arguments**— values passed to the function when it's called—those would go between the parentheses.

check for Ajax support p. 28

- The **ajax.js** file, which defines the **getXMLHttpRequestObject()** function, is the most important script in any Ajax application. The function returns either a valid, browser-safe **XMLHttpRequest** object or the value **false**. If it returns the object, that object contains all the functionality required to perform an Ajax transaction.

- The latest versions of most browsers support the **XMLHttpRequest object**. Due to its increasing popularity, this should remain so, even though it's not part of any standard at the time of this writing.

- Internet Explorer versions 5 and 6 didn't support a Java-Script **XMLHttpRequest** object. Instead they supported an **ActiveX** object of type **XMLHTTP**. Unfortunately, if users with one of these versions of Internet Explorer have disabled ActiveX support (enabling it is a security risk), they cannot use Ajax-enabled applications like these.

extra bits (cont.)

call the function p. 29

- The **window.onload** property tells the JavaScript the name of the function to call once the page has completely loaded. In this case that's **init**, short for **initialize** (i.e., set things up).

- The benefit of calling the initialization function in this way (rather than just calling it directly) is that the downloading and drawing of the page in the Web browser won't have to wait for the JavaScript to do its thing. In a slight way, this makes for a better user experience.

set up the Ajax p. 30

- The JavaScript refers to the **Document Object Model** to access elements in the HTML page. The DOM is a map of every item in a browser document. It can be used and manipulated in limitless ways.

- The **getElementById()** function allows you to access a DOM element by referring to its **ID** value. So a form with an ID of **dept_form** can be accessed via **document.getElementById('dept_form')**.

- Remember that the **ajax** variable is an object of **XMLHttpRequest** type. One of its functions is **open()**. Provide this function with the name of the page where

the request should be sent and the method that should be used.

- Because the PHP script that handles the request expects to receive a department ID in the URL, the value selected in the HTML form must be passed along with the request. You can access that value using the DOM.

- The **encodeURIComponent()** function ensures that the selected form value is safe to send in a URL.

- In this JavaScript code there are two **anonymous functions**. These are functions not given a name when defined. Anonymous functions are used when it's necessary to encapsulate a chunk of code but it's not necessary to call that code like a standard function.

- The XMLHttpRequest **readyState** value stores the current Ajax transaction state, on a scale from 0 to 4. The most important of these is 4, which means that the transaction is complete.

print the employees p. 33

- This PHP script is almost exactly like **dept_results.php** from Chapter 2. The main difference is that it does not include the opening and closing **<html>**, **<head>**, and **<body>** tags, nor does it include most of the stuff that goes within those tags. The reason why is that all of this page's results will be inserted into the HTML page via JavaScript. That page already has the proper HTML tags.

handle the response p. 35

- In the **init()** function, we tell the JavaScript to call a function called **handleResponse()** whenever the **readyState** value changes. This value will change multiple times during an Ajax request, so this function will be called multiple times.

- The **XMLHttpRequest status** attribute stores the **HTTP status code** returned by the server-side page. There are dozens of status codes from **200**, meaning that everything was OK, to values over 500, which are normally server errors. A status code of **304** indicates that the page was found but had not been modified since a certain date and time.

For the purposes of these examples, we'll assume it means the response was fine.

- By referring to the Document Object Model, we can forcibly submit the form. The **document. getElementById('dept_ form')** code refers to the form (which has an **id** value of **dept_ form**). The **.submit()** part of the code submits it.

display the results p. 36

- Once again, the Document Object Model allows you to easily access individual elements in a page. The code **document. getElementById('results')** refers to a **div** in the HTML page that has an **id** of **results**.

- The Cascading Style Sheet **style.css** sets the **display** attrbute of items with an **id** of **results** to **none**. The net effect will be that such elements are not visible when a page is first loaded. This is desired because such items have a solid green border around them and it'd be distracting to see that prior to actually retrieving the results.

extra bits (cont.)

- The process of hiding, then showing the results area using CSS and JavaScript is intended to make it more obvious when the HTML page is updated.

- Referring to an element's **innerHTML** value is a quick way to place next text on a page. An alternative is to add **nodes** to the DOM. You'll see this in Chapter 7, "enabling an Ajax search."

test the Ajax layer p. 38

- Debugging Ajax applications can be particularly tricky because there are so many technologies involved: HTML, DOM, CSS, JavaScript, PHP, SQL, and MySQL. See Appendix A, "where to go from here," for debugging tips.

- You'll want to test any Ajax application in as many Web browsers on as many operating systems as possible. By knowing how the application behaves under multiple settings, you do your best to avoid exluding any users.

- Firefox is, in my opinion, the best browser to test Ajax applications in. It has a JavaScript console that opens in another window for displaying JavaScript errors. This alone can be a great help.

4. adding records

In the first chapter we created the database structure for this employee listing Web site. In the previous two chapters, we developed an Ajax as well as a non-Ajax approach for browsing the employees by department. In this chapter, let's create a way to add employees to the database. Naturally we'll start with the non-Ajax version, for universal accessiblity, and then add the Ajax-enabled version in the next chapter.

To begin, we'll start by creating the **HTML form** that takes all the requisite data. Then we'll write the **PHP script** that handles the form submission in a non-Ajax way. This will all be fairly basic PHP form handling.

what we'll do

1 First, on pages 45-48, we'll create an **HTML page with a form**.

The form has elements ———— representing all of the data that's stored in the database for each employee.

On non-Ajax-enabled browers, when the user clicks **Add**, the form will be submitted to a PHP script.

2 On pages 49-54, the **PHP script** that handles the HTML form will be written. The **script validates the form data** and reports on the results.

If any fields weren't properly ———— filled out, the PHP script prints an error message.

Use this form to add an employee (all fields are required):

FIRST NAME [   ]

LAST NAME [   ]

EMAIL ADDRESS [   ]

DEPARTMENT [Human Resources   ▾]

PHONE EXTENSION [   ]

[Add]

Add an Employee

The following errors occurred:

- Please enter a valid first name.
- Please enter a valid last name.
- Please enter a valid email address.
- Please enter a valid phone extension.

3 Naturally, we'll **test** what we've built to make sure it all works.

At the end of this chapter, in the **extra bits** section, you'll find more information, tips, and recommendations regarding all these steps.

In the next chapter, we'll add the Ajax layer to these pages.

start the HTML page

Start by creating a **new HTML page** in your HTML editor.

```
<!DOCTYPE html PUBLIC "-//W3C//DTD XHTML 1.0 Strict//
EN"
"http://www.w3.org/TR/xhtml1/DTD/xhtml1-strict.dtd">
<html xmlns="http://www.w3.org/1999/xhtml" xml:
lang="en" lang="en">
<head>
  <meta http-equiv="content-type" content="text/html;
charset=utf-8" />
  <title>Add an Employee</title>
  <style type="text/css" media="all">@import "style.
css";</style>
</head>
<body>
</body>
</html>
```

The **title** will reflect what this page is for.

The **style sheet** will give this page the same look as the other pages in the site.

adding records

add the form

1 **Add a message** indicating what the form is for and how it should be used.

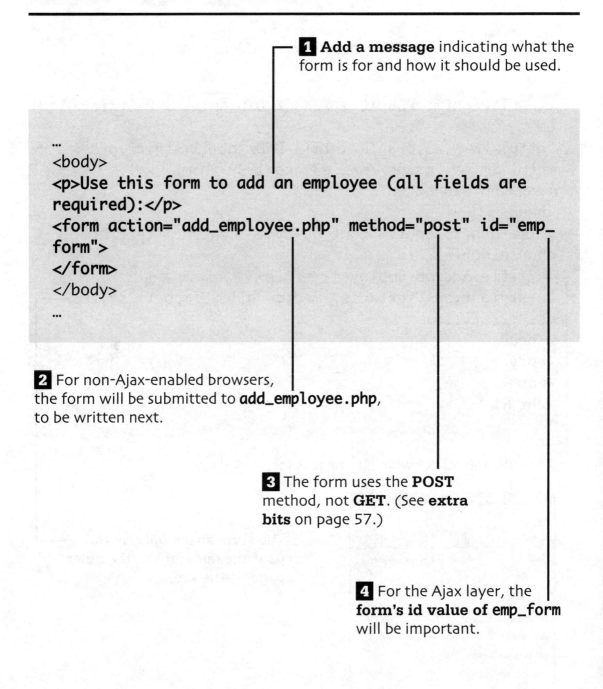

```
...
<body>
<p>Use this form to add an employee (all fields are
required):</p>
<form action="add_employee.php" method="post" id="emp_
form">
</form>
</body>
...
```

2 For non-Ajax-enabled browsers, the form will be submitted to **add_employee.php**, to be written next.

3 The form uses the **POST** method, not **GET**. (See **extra bits** on page 57.)

4 For the Ajax layer, the **form's id value of emp_form** will be important.

adding records

add the form elements

1 **Text inputs** take the employee's first name, last name, and email address.

```
...
<form action="add_employee.php" method="post" id="emp_
form">
<p><label class="title" id="first_name_label">First Name
<input type="text" id="first_name" name="first_name"
/></label> </p>
<p><label class="title" id="last_name_label">Last Name
<input type="text" id="last_name" name="last_name" /></
label> </p>
<p><label class="title" id="email_label">Email Address
<input type="text" id="email" name="email" /></label>
</p>
```

add the form elements

2 A **drop-down menu** will allow the user to select the employee's department.

```
<p><label class="title" id="department_id_
label">Department <select id="department_id"
name="department_id">
   <option value="1">Human Resources</option>
   <option value="2">Accounting</option>
   <option value="3">Marketing</option>
   <option value="4">Redundancy Department</option>
</select></label> </p>
```

3 Another text input is for the employee's phone extension.

```
<p><label class="title" id="phone_ext_label">Phone
Extension <input type="text" id="phone_ext" name="phone_
ext" /></label> </p>
<p><input name="add" type="submit" value="Add" /></p>
</form>
...
```

4 Labels are added to indicate what each element is for. (See **extra bits** on page 57.)

5 The **submit button** has a value of **Add**.

6 Save this file as **add_employee. html** and place it in the same directory as all the other site pages.

FIRST NAME	
LAST NAME	
EMAIL ADDRESS	
DEPARTMENT	Human Resources
	Human Resources
	Accounting
	Marketing
	Redundancy Department
PHONE EXTEN	
Add	

start a PHP page

The first PHP page handles the non-Ajax form submission. It should also be a valid HTML document, so start with those tags.

```
<!DOCTYPE html PUBLIC "-//W3C//DTD XHTML 1.0 Strict//EN"
 "http://www.w3.org/TR/xhtml1/DTD/xhtml1-strict.dtd">
<html xmlns="http://www.w3.org/1999/xhtml" xml:lang="en"
lang="en">
<head>
  <meta http-equiv="content-type" content="text/html;
charset=utf-8" />
  <title>Add an Employee</title>
  <style type="text/css" media="all">@import "style.
css";</style>
</head>
<body>
<h1>Add an Employee</h1>
<?php # add_employee.php
require_once('mysql.inc.php');
mysql_close($dbc);
?>
</body>
</html>
```

All of the page's functionality will go in between the PHP tags.

This page will need to communicate with MySQL, so the **mysql.inc.php** script must be included.

The MySQL connection is closed before the script terminates.

This file must be saved as **add_employee.php** and placed in the same directory as **add_employee**.html.

validate the form data

The form data must be validated prior to using it in a query. Add this code to the PHP page:

```php
...
require_once('mysql.inc.php');
$errors = array();
if (!empty($_POST['first_name'])) {
   $fn = mysql_real_escape_string($_POST['first_name'],
$dbc);
} else {
   $errors[] = 'first name';
}
```

1 The **$errors array will store any errors** encountered while validating the form.

2 Text inputs will be validated by **confirming that they aren't empty**. (See **extra bits** on page 57.)

```php
if (!empty($_POST['last_name'])) {
   $ln = mysql_real_escape_string($_POST['last_name'],
$dbc);
} else {
   $errors[] = 'last name';
}
```

adding records

```
if (!empty($_POST['email'])) {
  $e = mysql_real_escape_string($_POST['email'],
$dbc);
} else {
  $errors[] = 'email address';
}
```

3 To make sure the data is safe to use in
a query, text inputs are run through the
mysql_real_escape_string() function.

validate the form data (cont.)

```
if (isset($_POST['department_id']) && is_numeric($_
POST['department_id']) && ($_POST['department_id'] >
0)) {
   $did = (int) $_POST['department_id'];
} else {
   $errors[] = 'department';
}
```

4 **Numeric values**, like the department ID and the phone extension, **must be positive numbers**.

```
if (isset($_POST['phone_ext']) && is_numeric($_
POST['phone_ext']) && ($_POST['phone_ext'] > 0)) {
   $ext = (int) $_POST['phone_ext'];
} else {
   $errors[] = 'phone extension';
}
mysql_close($dbc);
…
```

5 To make them safe to use in a query, **numeric values are type-cast** as integers.

6 Any failed validation routine results in an element being added to the **$errors** array.

update the database

Assuming that the form data passed all the validation routines, an **INSERT** query should be run.

1 If there were no errors, this conditional will be true (because the **$errors** variable will be empty).

```
...
  $errors[] = 'phone extension';
}
if (!$errors) {
  $q = "INSERT INTO employees VALUES (NULL, $did,
'$fn', '$ln', '$e', $ext)";
  $r = mysql_query($q, $dbc);
  if (mysql_affected_rows($dbc) == 1) {
    echo '<p><strong>The employee has been added.</
strong></p>';
mysql_close($dbc);
...
```

2 The **INSERT** query adds the new employee to the database using the purified data from the validation routines. (See **extra bits** on page 58.)

3 The **mysql_affected_rows()** function returns the number of, well, affected rows. For this script's query, the number of affected rows should be 1, as one new record should be added.

4 The results are reported to the user. ————

adding records

report any errors

Finally, indicate to the user what problems occurred, if applicable.

1 The first **else** clause applies if the query did not result in one affected row. This would normally be the result of a syntax error. (See **extra bits** on page 58.)

```
...
    echo '<p><strong>The employee has been added.</strong></p>';
} else { // Query failure.
    echo '<p class="error">The employee could not be added due to a system error.</p>';
}
} else { // Errors!
    echo '<p>The following errors occurred:</p><ul class="error">';
    foreach ($errors as $e) {
        echo "<li>Please enter a valid $e.</li>\n";
    }
    echo '</ul>';
}
mysql_close($dbc);
...
```

2 The second **else** clause applies if the data didn't pass all the validation tests.

3 Because the errors are stored in an array, looping through them is the easiest way to access them all.

Add an Employee

The following errors occurred:

- Please enter a valid first name.
- Please enter a valid last name.
- Please enter a valid email address.
- Please enter a valid phone extension.

test the non-Ajax version

1 **Load the HTML page** in your Web browser to test what we've created so far.

The address **must begin with http://** for this to work.

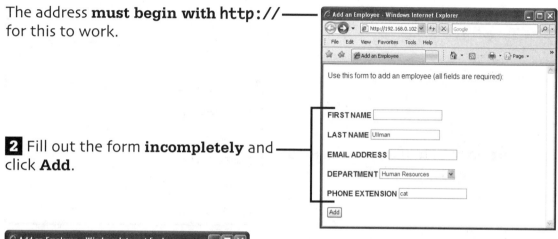

2 Fill out the form **incompletely** and click **Add**.

3 The PHP page should show the results.

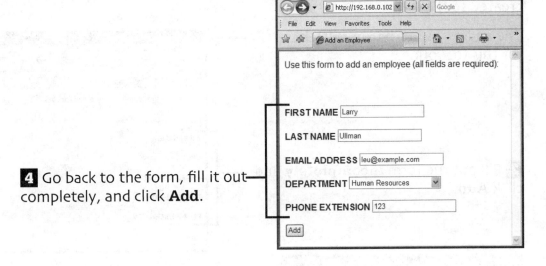

4 Go back to the form, fill it out completely, and click **Add**.

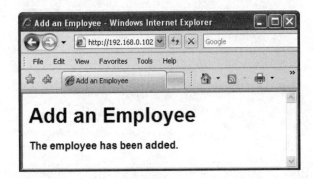

5 Again, the PHP page shows the results.

extra bits

add the form p. 46

- The **POST** method should generally be used when the form's submission should have an effect on the site. For example, using the Add an Employee form adds another record to the database.

- The **GET** method should generally be used when requesting information. For example, you should apply it when requesting the employees in a specific department.

add the form elements p. 47

- The form's labels will serve two purposes. First, they indicate to the user what each form element is for. Second, they'll be modified, using JavaScript, to indicate an error in the Ajax-enabled version of this form.

validate the form data p. 50

- How you validate form data depends on the data's type (numbers, strings, etc.) and expected values (positive number, email address, and so on). For validating a person's name, it's often sufficient to make sure that some value is entered.

- A more thorough validation of an email address would be to confirm that it matches a **regular expression pattern**. You can do this with email addresses more so than names because they must abide by strict rules.

- You could improve the security of this system by applying PHP's `strip_tags()` function to the text inputs. That function can help prevent cross-site scripting attacks (XSS).

- The `mysql_real_escape_string()` function provides language-specific protection on text used in queries.

update the database p. 53

- A more precise way to write the **INSERT** query would be to use the syntax where you specify the columns involved. For this query, that would be **INSERT INTO employees (department_id, first_name, last_name, email, phone_ext) VALUES ($did, '$fn', '$ln', '$e', $ext)**.

report any errors p. 54

- To debug any PHP–MySQL problems, you'll need to **print out the query** to inspect its syntax. You should also invoke the **mysql_error()** function to see what problems the database reports.

- Live sites should never provide detailed behind-the-scenes errors, such as the queries being run or the MySQL errors. Use this information for debugging purposes, and then hide that information in the live version (which, we hope, shouldn't encounter such errors).

5. adding records via Ajax

In the previous chapter, we created a way to add employees to the database. That process required one HTML form and one PHP script that handled the form. It all works fine but in the old-fashioned, client-server kind of way.

In this chapter, let's set an Ajax layer on top of those scripts so that, for the browsers that support it, our form for adding employees can behave more like a desktop application. To do so, we'll need to **slightly modify the HTML page**. Then we'll create **one JavaScript file** that has the page-specific Ajax functionality. Finally, a **new PHP script** will be written that handles the Ajax request.

This example will also introduce two new techniques: sending an Ajax request **using the POST method** and **working with XML data**. This Ajax example is a little more complicated than the previous one, but it should all make sense by the end of the chapter.

what we'll do

1 First, on pages 62, we'll **modify the HTML page** to include the necessary Ajax pieces.

2 On Ajax-enabled browers, when the user clicks **Add**, the page-specific JavaScript will read in all the form data and submit it to a new PHP script. On pages 63-66, we'll begin the **JavaScript file** that starts this process.

3 The **PHP script**, written on pages 67-74, will validate all the data and report on the results. Its response will be returned as XML.

4 The JavaScript will take the **XML returned by the PHP script** and use it to update the HTML page. We'll complete this file on pages 75-79.

5 Naturally, we'll **test** what we've built to make sure it all works.

6 At the end of this chapter, in the **extra bits** section, you'll find more information, tips, and recommendations regarding all of these steps.

HTML page

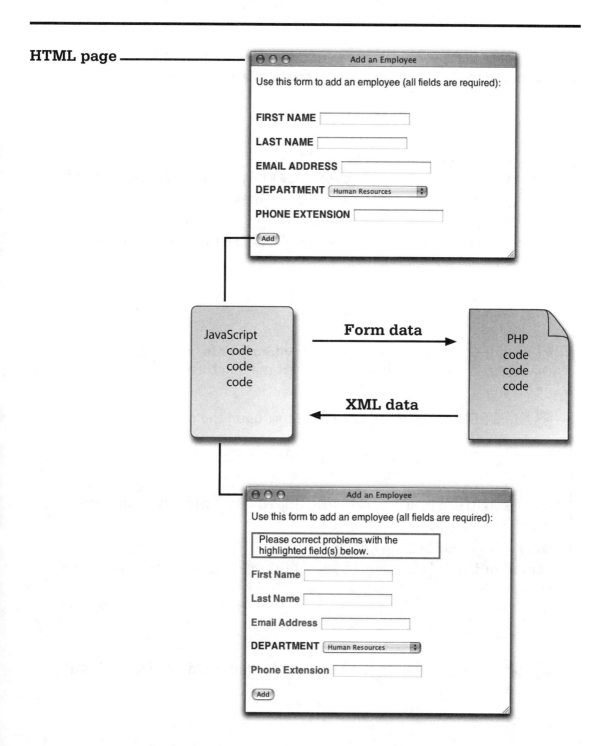

adding records via Ajax

add the Ajax elements

1 Include the **generic Ajax JavaScript file** by adding the right code to the HTML head. (See **extra bits** on page 82.)

```
...
<title>Add an Employee</title>
<script src="ajax.js" type="text/javascript"></script>
<script src="add_employee.js" type="text/
javascript"></script>
<style type="text/css" media="all">@import "style.
css";</style>
...
```

2 Include the **page-specific Ajax JavaScript file** by adding that code to the HTML head. We'll start making this script next.

3 Add a **DIV** to the HTML page to report upon the results.

```
...
<p>Use this form to add an employee (all fields are
required):</p>
<div id="results"></div>
<form action="add_employee.php" method="post" id="emp_
form">
...
```

4 Save the file (it will continue to use the name **add_employee.html**).

apply the Ajax layer

Create a new JavaScript file that starts with the following code (see **extra bits** on page 82):

1 The first line tells the Web browser to run the **init()** function after loading the entire page. The **init()** function sets up all the Ajax activity.

```
window.onload = init;
function init() {
    var ajax = getXMLHttpRequestObject();
```

2 The function calls the **getXML-HttpRequestObject()** function to get a valid, browser-specific object. This function is defined in **ajax.js**, which will have already been included by the HTML page.

3 The function then checks to see if the **ajax** variable has a valid value. With supported browsers, **ajax** will be an **XMLHttpRequest** object. With nonsupported browsers, **ajax** will have a value of **false**, and this conditional will be false.

```
if (ajax) {
    if (document.getElementById('results')) {
        document.getElementById('emp_form').onsubmit =
function() {
```

4 Next, the function checks to see if the browser supports the **document object model (DOM)** and, specifically, if the page has an element with an **id** of **results**.

5 Finally, an **onsubmit()** event is attached to the form (which has an **id** value of **emp_form**). In other words, when the form is submitted, do the following....

set up the Ajax

```
...
document.getElementById('emp_form').onsubmit =
function() {
    ajax.open('post', 'add_employee_xml.php');
    ajax.onreadystatechange = function() {
        handleResponse(ajax);
    }
```

1 Tell the **ajax** object that you want to use the **POST method**. (See **extra bits** on page 82.)

2 Provide to the **ajax** object the name of the page that should be sent the request. This is **add_employee_xml.php**, to be written next.

3 When the **ajax** object's **readyState** value changes, the **handleResponse()** function should be called, passing that function this same object.

prepare the form data

1 The **fields** variable is an array of the form elements whose values need to be sent to the PHP page.

2 Loop through each element in the array.

3 In the loop, each array element will be turned into a string in the format **name=value**. So the first array element, **first_name**, will be turned into something like **first_name=Larry**. (See **extra bits** on page 83.)

```
...
   handleResponse(ajax);
}
var fields = ['first_name', 'last_name', 'email',
'department_id','phone_ext'];
for (var i = 0; i < fields.length; i++) {
   fields[i] = fields[i] + '=' +
encodeURIComponent(document.getElementById(fields[i]).
value);
}
var values = fields.join('&');
ajax.setRequestHeader('Content-Type', 'application/x-
www-form-urlencoded');
```

4 In the loop, each form element's value is retrieved using the Document Object Model. The value is run through the **encodeURIComponent()** function for security purposes.

5 Outside of the loop, all of the array elements (the **name=value** pairs) are joined together with ampersands. The end result is a string like **first_name=Larry&last_name=Ullman&...**

6 The **Content-Type** header indicates what kind of information is about to be sent. The value **application/x-www-form-urlencoded** means that the content is encoded form data.

complete the function

1 After all the data handling, the actual Ajax request is made. The form data, represented by the variable **values**, is used as the only argument to the **send()** method. (See **extra bits** on page 83.)

```
...
        ajax.setRequestHeader('Content-Type',
'application/x-www-form-urlencoded');
        ajax.send(values);
        return false;
      } // End of anonymous function.
    } // End of DOM check.
  } // End of ajax IF.
} // End of init() function.
```

2 Finally, the function returns a value of **false** to tell the Web browser not to actually submit the form (since Ajax is handling the form submission).

Save this file as **add_employee.js** and place it in the same directory on your Web server as every other file.

prepare for XML

A new PHP script will do the same thing as **add_employee.php**, only it will return all of its results as XML data. This data will be handled by the JavaScript in the Web browser. Start a new PHP script in your text-editing application.

1 This PHP page will not be viewed in the Web browser, so it begins with the opening PHP tag, not with HTML. (See **extra bits** on page 83.)

2 The **header()** function is used to send meta-information (i.e., not actual data). Here the **header()** function sends a **Content-Type** of **text/xml**. In layman's terms, this is a way of saying that XML data should be expected to follow.

```php
<?php # add_employee_xml.php
header("Content-Type: text/xml");
echo '<?xml version="1.0" encoding="utf-8"
standalone="yes" ?>
<response>
';
```

3 XML data begins wth the **declaration**.

4 All XML documents have **one root element.** This can be a made-up value, like **response** here.

validate the form data

The form data must be validated prior to using it in a query. Add this code to the PHP page.

1 The **$error variable will be a flag**, indicating if an error occurred.

```
…
<response>
';
require_once('mysql.inc.php');
$error = false;
if (!empty($_POST['first_name'])) {
```

2 Text inputs will be validated by **confirming that they aren't empty**. (See **extra bits** on page 84.)

3 To make sure the data is safe to use in a query, text inputs are run through the **mysql_real_escape_string()** function.

```
   $fn = mysql_real_escape_string($_POST['first_name'],
$dbc);
} else {
  $error = true;
  echo '<error>first_name</error>
';
}
if (!empty($_POST['last_name'])) {
  $ln = mysql_real_escape_string($_POST['last_name'],
```

```
} else {
  $error = true;
  echo '<error>last_name</error>
';
}
if (!empty($_POST['email'])) {
  $e = mysql_real_escape_string($_POST['email'],
$dbc);
} else {
  $error = true;
  echo '<error>email</error>
';
}
```

4 **Numeric values**, like the department ID and the phone extension, **must be positive numbers**.

5 To make them safe to use in a query, **numeric values are type-cast** as integers.

```
if (isset($_POST['department_id']) && is_numeric($_
POST['department_id']) && ($_POST['department_id'] >
0)) {
  $did = (int) $_POST['department_id'];
} else {
  $error = true;
  echo '<error>department_id</error>
';
}
if (isset($_POST['phone_ext']) && is_numeric($_
POST['phone_ext']) && ($_POST['phone_ext'] > 0)) {
  $ext = (int) $_POST['phone_ext'];
} else {
  $error = true;
  echo '<error>phone_ext</error>
';
}
```

6 Any failed validation routine results in the **$error** variable being set to **true**.

7 To report the error back to the JavaScript, an XML element is created with a name of **error**. The value of the XML element is the name of the form element improperly filled out.

update the database

Assuming that the form data passed all the validation routines, an **INSERT** query should be run.

1 If there were no errors, then this conditional will be true (because the **$error** variable will be false).

2 The **INSERT** query adds the new employee to the database using the purified data from the validation routines.

```
...
echo '<error>phone_ext</error>
';
}
if (!$error) {
    $q = "INSERT INTO employees VALUES (NULL, $did,
'$fn', '$ln', '$e', $ext)";
    $r = mysql_query($q, $dbc);
    if (mysql_affected_rows($dbc) == 1) {
        echo '<result>The employee has been added.</result>';
```

3 The **mysql_affected_rows()** function returns the number of, well, affected rows. This should be 1, as one new record should be added.

```
- <response>
      <result>The employee has been added.</result>
  </response>
```

4 The results are added to the XML output, using an element name of **result**.

complete the XML

1 The first **else** clause applies if the query did not result in one affected row. A syntax error would typically be the cause. (See **extra bits** on page 84.)

2 The second **else** clause applies if the data didn't pass all the validation tests.

```
...
    echo '<result>The employee has been added.</
result>';
  } else { // Query failure.
    echo '<result>The employee could not be added due
to a system error.</result>
';
  }
} else { // Errors!
  echo '<result>Please correct problems with the
highlighted field(s) below.</result>
';
}
```

adding records via Ajax   **73**

```
mysql_close($dbc);
echo '</response>';
?>
```

```
- <response>
    <error>first_name</error>
    <error>last_name</error>
    <error>email</error>
    <error>phone_ext</error>
  - <result>
      Please correct problems with the highlighted field(s) below.
    </result>
  </response>
```

3 For both **else** clauses, an appropriately descriptive message is included in the XML output, within an element called **result**.

4 Close the root XML element to complete the XML output. No need to use closing HTML tags!

handle the response

The PHP page sends back XML data, which must be handled by the JavaScript. Add this new function to the **add_employee.js** JavaScript file. (See **extra bits** on page 85.)

1 This JavaScript function is called when the **ajax** object's **readyState** value changes (see the **init()** function). The function receives the **ajax** object when called.

```
function handleResponse(ajax) {
   if (ajax.readyState == 4) {
      if ((ajax.status == 200) || (ajax.status == 304) )
   {
```

2 The function shouldn't do anything until **readyState** has a value of 4, meaning that the Ajax transaction is complete.

3 If the **status** code is equal to either 200 or 304, we can use the returned results.

prepare the page

1 The **results** variable now refers to a specific area in the DOM (Document Object Model) of the HTML page.

```
...
if ((ajax.status == 200) || (ajax.status == 304) ) {
    var results = document.getElementById('results');
    document.getElementById('first_name_label').
className = 'title';
    document.getElementById('last_name_label').className
= 'title';
      document.getElementById('email_label').className =
'title';
      document.getElementById('department_id_label').
className = 'title';
    document.getElementById('phone_ext_label').className
= 'title';
```

2 Each of the form's labels should have its class reset to the default class of **title**. (See **extra bits** on page 85.)

handle the XML

1 The XML data returned by the PHP script can be accessed via **ajax.responseXML**, which we assign to a variable called **data**. (See **extra bits** on page 86.)

2 The variable **message** will refer to the XML element with a tag name of **result**.

```
…
document.getElementById('phone_ext_label').className =
'title';
var data = ajax.responseXML;
var message = data.getElementsByTagName('result');
var errors = data.getElementsByTagName('error');
var temp = false;
```

3 The variable **errors** will refer to every XML element with a tag name of **error**.

handle the XML (cont.)

4 Loop through the **errors** array to access every one.

```
for (var i = 0; i < errors.length; i++) {
  temp = errors[i].firstChild.nodeValue;
  document.getElementById(temp + '_label').className =
'error';
}
```

5 A temporary variable will be assigned the value of the error from the XML data.

6 The error value is used to change the class of the corresponding form label.

FIRST NAME Larry

Last Name

Email Address

DEPARTMENT Human Resources

adding records via Ajax

display the results

The final step in the Ajax process is to display the results message by placing that message on the HTML page. This code completes the **handleResponse()** function. (See **extra bits** on page 86.)

1 The text in the **results** area is set to the returned response from the Ajax request.

```
...
document.getElementById(temp + '_label').className =
'error';
        }
        results.innerHTML = message[0].firstChild.
nodeValue;
        results.style.display = 'block';
    } else {
        document.getElementById('emp_form').submit();
    }
  } // End of readyState IF.
} // End of handleResponse() function.
```

2 Because the **results** area is initially invisible, we need to make it visible now that we have some results to display.

3 If we didn't get a valid status code back from the Ajax request, we should formally submit the form to the handling PHP page (as if the Ajax layer didn't exist at all).

Use this form to add an employee (all fields are required):

Please correct problems with the highlighted field(s) below.

FIRST NAME Larry

test the Ajax layer

1 **Load the HTML page** in your Web browser.

The address **must begin with http://** for this to work.

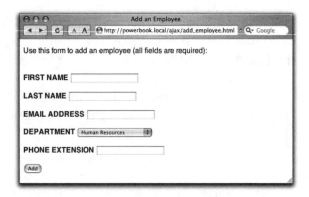

2 Fill out the form **incompletely** or **improperly** and click **Add**.

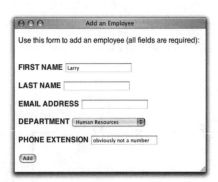

3 The HTML page should show the results without reloading the page or going to a new page.

4 Fill out the form completely and click **Add**.

5 Again, the HTML page shows the results.

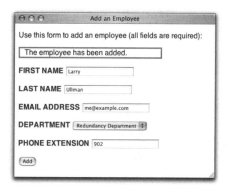

extra bits

add the Ajax elements p. 62

- The **ajax.js** file, written in Chapter 3, "browsing using Ajax," defines a function that returns a **browser-specific XMLHttpRequest object**. This file is needed by any page that performs any Ajax operations.

- Because the **DIV**, where the results will be reported, has an **id value of results**, it will be formatted according to the rules dictated in **style.css**. This is the same as the **results DIV in dept_form.html**. For starters, the **DIV** will be hidden when the page is first viewed.

apply the Ajax layer p. 63

- Most of this code is exactly like that in **dept.js**. You'll find that to be the case with a good Ajax base, like the one we've developed in this book. The only change in this first bit of code is the reference to **emp_form**. It's in the rest of the code—what should be done when the form is submitted—that the big differences can be found.

set up the Ajax p. 64

- The **POST** method should generally be used when the form's submission should have an effect on the site. For example, using the add-an-employee form adds another record to the database.

- The **GET** method should generally be used when requesting information—for example, when requesting the employees in a specific department.

adding records via Ajax

prepare the form data p. 65

- When a form is submitted using the **GET** method, you'll see the form data in the URL, with a syntax of `page.php?this_item=this_value&that_item=that_value`. This is the same syntax used by **POST**, but the data isn't sent in the URL and you don't need the question mark.

- All of the form data needs to be run through the **encodeURIComponent()** function to make it safe to send to the PHP page. Rather than apply that function to each value separately, using a **for** loop on an array of form elements lets us accomplish the same thing with less code.

- The **plus sign in JavaScript** is used to perform **concatenation**: appending one string onto another. In PHP, the period does the same thing.

- If you wanted to send XML data to the PHP script, you would set the **Content-Type** to **text/xml**.

complete the function p. 66

- When using the GET method, use the value null as the only argument when calling **send()**. Any data sent over GET is appended to the URL itself. When using POST, you need to provide the data when you call **send()**, as it's not sent in the URL.

prepare for XML p. 67

- The PHP script sends its response as XML data, not as a normal Web page. Everything PHP will print will be part of this XML.

- The XML data being created is really like the data in an HTML page, where there's one root element and any number of nested subelements. For this example, the root element will be called **response** and there will be two subelements. There can be zero or more elements called **error** and there will always be exactly one element called **result**. In comparison, an HTML page has a root element called **html**, two subelements named **head** and **body**, and more subelements within those.

extra bits (cont.)

- If the PHP page does not use the **header()** function to set the **Content-Type**, the JavaScript that receives this response will not recognize it as XML.

- You don't have to fully understand XML to do this example or to use XML in general. But should you want to better understand the subject, search the Web for more information.

validate the form data p. 68

- For more information on the form validation routines, see the extra bits section for Chapter 4, "adding records."

- The XML data will have zero or more elements called **error**. Any failed validation will result in another **error** element, whose value will match the name of the corresponding form field. The point of this XML data is to indicate which form fields weren't properly filled out. If all of the validation tests were passed, there will be none of these elements.

complete the XML p. 73

- To debug any PHP-MySQL problems, you'll need to **print out the query** to inspect its syntax. You should also invoke the **mysql_error()** function to see what problems the database reports.

- A useful debugging technique when working with XML data is to verify that your PHP script is returning valid XML. To see the result of the PHP page, either use JavaScript to access **ajax.responseText** (in the **handleResponse()** function) or submit your form to the PHP page directly (without using JavaScript).

- For directly viewing XML in your Web browser, you'll want to use a browser that supports the format. At the time of this writing, this includes recent versions of Internet Explorer and Firefox, but not Safari.

handle the response p. 75

- In the **init()** function, we tell the JavaScript to call a function called **handleResponse()** whenever the **readyState** value changes. This value will change multiple times during an Ajax request, so this function will be called multiple times.

- The XMLHttpRequest **status** attribute stores the **HTTP status code** returned by the server-side page. There are dozens of status codes—from **200**, meaning that everything was OK, to values over 500, which are normally server errors. A status code of **304** indicates that the page was found but had not been modified since a certain date and time.

prepare the page p. 76

- One of the new tricks in this chapter's example is that the form elements' labels will be changed to indicate errors. Specifically, any problematic field will have its label class switched from the default **title** to **error**. Upon a resubmission of the form, the labels should have their class values reset so that they can reflect the new results.

extra bits (cont.)

handle the XML p. 77

- The server's response is available in two attributes of the XMLHttpRequest object. It can be found as plain text in **responseText** or as XML data in **responseXML**.

- The XML data can be accessed just like an HTML page, using the Document Object Model. So **data.getElementsByTagName ('error')** refers to every item in the XML data with a name of **error**.

- The syntax of the **for** loop is a common way to access every item found in an array. Within the loop, the specific array item is accessed via **arrayname[i]**.

- The error elements in the XML data have the names of the problematic form elements as their values. To access these values, refer to the error element, which is **errors[i]** within the loop, followed by **.firstChild. nodeValue**. It's a rather complex syntax but it works. More information on a **child** and a **node** can be found in Chapter 7, "enabling an Ajax search."

- To indicate a problem with a form element, its corresponding label will have its class changed from **title** to **error**. Using the Document Object Model, **document.getElement-ById(temp + '_label')** will refer to the label (where **temp** stores the name of the form element). Then **.className** lets you change its class.

display the results p. 79

- The **message** variable refers to every XML element with a name of **result** (see the code earlier in the function). Even though the XML data will only ever have one such element, an array is still returned. So the text itself is accessed via the unwieldy **message[0].firstChild.nodeValue**.

- As with the previous Ajax example, the **innerHTML** property is used to put a message within the **results DIV**.

adding records via Ajax

6. creating a search

Thus far in the book we've made two aspects of an employee-directory site. First, we created a way to browse employees by department. Then we made it possible to add employees to the database. Let's put in one last logical feature: the ablity to search for employees by last name.

In keeping with this book's approach, we'll start, in this chapter, with the non-Ajax version. These files will work for all users and give us a sense of what the process should entail. To create the search, we only need to put together two files: **one HTML form** and **one PHP script** that handles the form. Should be a snap!

what we'll do

1 First, on pages 89-91, we'll create an **HTML page with a form**.

The form has only one input: a text box where an employee's last name, or part thereof, can be entered.

> Enter the first letter or two of an employee's last name and click 'GO' to find matching employees.
>
> [Sh   ] [GO]

On non-Ajax-enabled browers, when the user clicks **GO**, the form will be submitted to a PHP script.

2 On pages 92-95, the **PHP script** that handles the HTML form will be written. The script uses the form data to perform a search on the database, printing the results.

Employee Search Results

SANDERS, JUSTINE
Department: Accounting
j.sanders@thiscompany.com

SMITH, LAILA
Department: Human Resources
l.smith@thiscompany.com

If no employees match the search term, the PHP script prints a message saying as much.

Employee Search Results

No employees were a match.

Naturally, we'll **test** what we've built to make sure it all works.

At the end of this chapter, in the **extra bits** section, you'll find more information, tips, and recommendations regarding all of these steps.

In the next chapter, we'll add the Ajax layer to these pages.

start the HTML page

Start by creating a **new HTML page** in your text editor.

```
<!DOCTYPE html PUBLIC "-//W3C//DTD XHTML 1.0 Strict//
EN"
"http://www.w3.org/TR/xhtml1/DTD/xhtml1-strict.dtd">
<html xmlns="http://www.w3.org/1999/xhtml" xml:
lang="en" lang="en">
<head>
  <meta http-equiv="content-type" content="text/html;
charset=utf-8" />
  <title>Search for Employees by Name</title>
<style type="text/css" media="all">@import "style.
css";</style>
</head>
<body>
<!-- search_form.html -->
</body>
</html>
```

The **title** reflects what this page is for.

The **style sheet** will give this page the same look as the other pages in the site.

Save the page as **search_form.html** and place it in the same
directory as all the other files from this book.

add the form

1 **Add a message** indicating what the form is for and how it should be used. (See **extra bits** on page 97.)

```
...
<!-- search_form.html -->
<p>Enter the first letter or two of an employee's last
name and click 'GO' to find matching employees.</p>
```

2 For non-Ajax-enabled browsers, the form will be submitted to **search_results.php**, to be written next.

3 The form uses the **GET method**, like **dept_form.html**.

```
<form action="search_results.php" method="get"
id="search_form">
<p><input    ="last_name" id="last_name" type="text"
size="5" maxlength="30" />
<input name="go" type="submit" value="GO" />
</p>
</form>
</body>
</html>
```

4 For the Ajax layer, the **form's id value of search_form** will be important.

start a PHP page

The **first PHP page** handles the non-Ajax form submission. It should also be a valid HTML document, so start with those tags.

```
<!DOCTYPE html PUBLIC "-//W3C//DTD XHTML 1.0 Strict//
EN"
"http://www.w3.org/TR/xhtml1/DTD/xhtml1-strict.dtd">
<html xmlns="http://www.w3.org/1999/xhtml" xml:
lang="en" lang="en">
<head>
  <meta http-equiv="content-type" content="text/html;
charset=utf-8" />
  <title>Search for Employees by Name</title>
  <style type="text/css" media="all">@import "style.
css";</style>
</head>
<body>
<h1>Employee Search Results</h1>
<?php # search_results.php
?>
</body>
</html>
```

All of the page's functionality will go in between the PHP tags.

This file must be saved as **search_results.php** and placed in the same directory as **search_form.html**.

query the database

1 We make sure that some value was submitted for the ⎯⎯⎯
last name or else there's no need to query the database.

2 The **MySQL connection** script is included.

```
...
<?php # search_results.php
if (!empty($_GET['last_name'])) {
    require_once('mysql.inc.php');
    $q = "SELECT CONCAT(last_name, ', ', first_name),
email, department FROM employees LEFT JOIN departments
USING (department_id) WHERE last_name LIKE '" . mysql_
real_escape_string($_GET['last_name']) . "%' ORDER BY
last_name, first_name";
    $r = mysql_query($q, $dbc);
?>
...
```

3 The query
will return every
employee's **name,
email address**,
and **department**
whose last name
begins with the
submitted letters.
(See **extra bits** on page 97.)

```
000                        Ajax
mysql> SELECT CONCAT(last_name, ', ', first_name), email, department FROM employees LEFT JOIN
   departments USING (department_id) WHERE last_name LIKE 'gr%' ORDER BY last_name, first_name;
+-----------------------------------------+-------------------------+------------------+
| CONCAT(last_name, ', ', first_name)     | email                   | department       |
+-----------------------------------------+-------------------------+------------------+
| Gray, Gideon                            | g.gray@thiscompany.com  | Accounting       |
| Green, Laverne                          | l.green@thiscompany.com | Human Resources  |
+-----------------------------------------+-------------------------+------------------+
2 rows in set (0.09 sec)

mysql>
```

4 The `mysql_real_escape_string()` function
makes it safe to use the submitted value in a query.

print the results

1 Check that **at least one record** was returned.

```
...
$r = mysql_query($q, $dbc);
if (mysql_num_rows($r) > 0) {
   while ($row = mysql_fetch_array($r, MYSQL_NUM)) {
      echo "<p><span class=\"name\">$row[0]</span><br />
      <strong>Department</strong>: $row[2]<br />
      <a href=\"mailto:$row[1]\">$row[1]</a>
      </p>\n";
   } // End of WHILE loop.
?>
...
```

2 **Fetch all the records** and print them out.

3 The employee's **name will be formatted** using a CSS class.

4 The employee's **email address will be linked** so that clicking on it begins an email to that person.

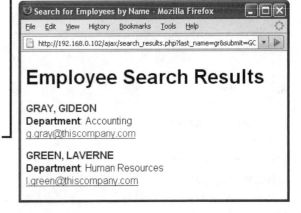

```
<h1>Employee Search Results</h1>
<p><span class="name">Gray, Gideon</span><br />
      <strong>Department</strong>: Accounting<br />
      <a href="mailto:g.gray@thiscompany.com">g.gray@thiscompany.com</a>
      </p>
<p><span class="name">Green, Laverne</span><br />
      <strong>Department</strong>: Human Resources<br />
      <a href="mailto:l.green@thiscompany.com">l.green@thiscompany.com</a>
      </p>
</body>
```

creating a search

report any errors

1 The first **else** clause applies if the query ran just fine but didn't return any results.

```
    } // End of WHILE loop.
  } else { // No employees.
    echo '<p class="error">No employees were a
match.</p>';
  }
  mysql_close($dbc);
} else { // Invalid form data!
  echo '<p class="error">Please enter at least a couple
of characters in the employee\'s last name.</p>';
}
?>
...
```

2 The **MySQL connection** is closed.

3 The second **else** clause applies if the form was not properly filled out.

Employee Search Results

Please enter at least a couple of characters in the employee's last name.

test the non-Ajax version

1 **Load the HTML page** in your Web browser to test what we've created so far.

The address **must begin with http://** for this to work.

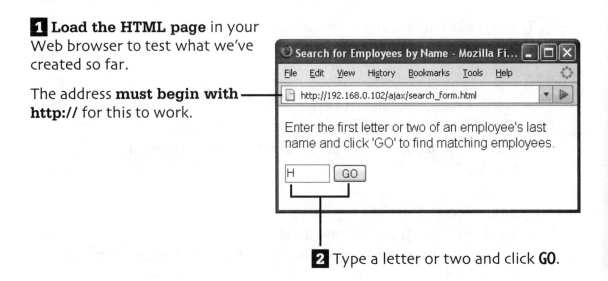

2 Type a letter or two and click **GO**.

3 The PHP page should show the **results**.

4 Go back to the form, and repeat Steps 2 and 3 until your heart's content.

extra bits

add the form p. 91

- In this example, I suggest that users only enter a couple of letters because the database only has 20 records in it. With the employees entered in Chapter 1, "creating the database," **Gr** will return two records but **Gre** only one. If your database had more names in it, entering longer values would be appropriate.

- The **GET** method is normally used with searches. The next time you use Google or some other search engine, notice that the search terms are passed along in the URL.

query the database p. 93

- This is the most complicated query in the book. It performs a **JOIN** across two tables: **employees** and **departments**, which are linked through the **department_id** columns. The search feature is possible thanks to a **LIKE** clause, asking for records where the employee's last name begins with whatever letters were entered in the form.

- Running a dynamically generated query through another interface, like the **mysql client** in the image, is a great debugging technique. Doing so will confirm what a query is, if it works, and what its results are.

7. enabling an Ajax search

As the last piece in this book's project, let's take the search created in the previous chapter and give it the old Ajax treatment. As in other chapters, we'll add an Ajax layer on top of what we've already created. Browsers that are Ajax-supportive will see the search results without reloading the page; every other browser will use the system already in place.

Accomplishing this will require **modifying the HTML page**. Then we'll need to make a **new JavaScript file** that contains all the functionality for this specific example. And a **new PHP script** will be written that returns the search results, in XML format, to the JavaScript. Unlike the other Ajax examples in this book, we won't use the `innerHTML` attribute in our JavaScript to update the Web page. Here, we'll add **nodes** to the **Document Object Model** as a way of manipulating the page's content.

what we'll do

1 First, on page 102, we'll **modify the HTML page** to include the necessary Ajax pieces.

2 The user enters the first couple of letters of the employee's last name and clicks **GO**. (See **extra bits** on page 124.)

3 On Ajax-enabled browers, the page-specific Java-Script will read in what the user typed and submit that to a new PHP script. On pages 103-106, we'll begin the **JavaScript file** that starts this process.

4 The **PHP script**, written on pages 107-110, will search the database for employees whose name begins with the provided letters. It will return any matched records as **XML data**.

5 The JavaScript will take the **XML returned by the PHP script** and use it to update the HTML page. We'll complete this JavaScript file on pages 111-122.

6 Naturally, we'll **test** what we've built on page 123 to make sure it all works.

7 At the end of this chapter, in the **extra bits** section, you'll find more information, tips, and recommendations regarding all of these steps.

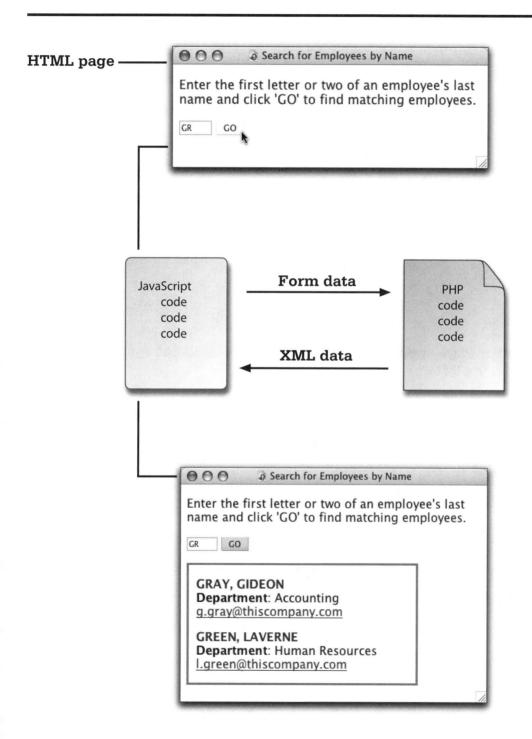

HTML page

Search for Employees by Name

Enter the first letter or two of an employee's last name and click 'GO' to find matching employees.

GR   GO

JavaScript
code
code
code

Form data →

PHP
code
code
code

← **XML data**

Search for Employees by Name

Enter the first letter or two of an employee's last name and click 'GO' to find matching employees.

GR   GO

GRAY, GIDEON
Department: Accounting
g.gray@thiscompany.com

GREEN, LAVERNE
Department: Human Resources
l.green@thiscompany.com

add the Ajax elements

1 Include the **generic Ajax JavaScript file** by adding the right code to the HTML head. (See **extra bits** on page 124.)

```
...
<title>Search for Employees by Name</title>
  <script src="ajax.js" type="text/javascript"></
script>
  <script src="search.js" type="text/javascript"></
script>
  <style type="text/css" media="all">@import "style.
css";</style>
...
```

2 Include the **page-specific Ajax JavaScript file** by adding that code to the HTML head. We'll start making this script next.

```
...
</form>
<div id="results"></div>
</body>
...
```

3 Add a **DIV** to the HTML page to report on the results.

4 Save the file (it will continue to use the name **search_form.html**).

apply the Ajax layer

Create a new JavaScript file that starts with the following code (see **extra bits** on page 124):

1 The first line tells the Web browsers to run the `init()` function after loading the entire page. The `init()` function sets up all the Ajax activity.

```
window.onload = init;
function init() {
    var ajax = getXMLHttpRequestObject();
    if (ajax) {
```

2 The function calls the **getXMLHttpRequestObject()** function to get a valid, browser-specific object. This function is defined in **ajax.js**, which will have already been included by the HTML page.

3 The function then checks to see if the **ajax** variable has a valid value. With supported browsers, **ajax** will be an **XMLHttpRequest** object. With nonsupported browsers, **ajax** will have a value of `false`, and this conditional will be false.

apply the Ajax layer (cont.)

4 Next, the function checks to see if the browser supports the **Document Object Model (DOM)** and, specifically, if the page has an element with an **id** of **results**.

```
if (document.getElementById('results')) {
    document.getElementById('search_form').onsubmit
= function() {
```

5 Finally, an **onsubmit()** event is attached to the form (which has an **id** value of **search_form**). In other words, when the form is submitted, do the following...

set up the Ajax

1 Provide to the **ajax** object the name of the page that should be sent the request. This is **search_results_xml.php**, to be written next. The request will be made using the **get** method.

```
...
document.getElementById('search_form').onsubmit =
function() {
  var last_name = document.getElementById('last_
name').value;
  ajax.open('get', 'search_results_xml.php?last_name='
+ encodeURIComponent(last_name));
  ajax.onreadystatechange = function() {
    handleResponse(ajax);
  }
```

2 As part of that request, the **last_name** value (the letters the user entered in the form) will be passed along in the URL. (See **extra bits** on page 124.)

3 When the **ajax** object's **readyState** value changes, the **handleResponse()** function should be called, passing that function this same object.

enabling an Ajax search

complete the function

1 The actual Ajax request is made.

2 Finally, the function returns a value of **false** to tell the Web browser not to actually submit the form (since the Ajax is handling the form submission).

```
...
        handleResponse(ajax);
      }
      ajax.send(null);
      return false;
     } // End of anonymous function.
    } // End of DOM check.
  } // End of ajax IF.
} // End of init() function.
```

Save this file as **search.js** and place it in the same directory on your Web server as every other file.

prepare for XML

A new PHP script will do the same thing as **search_results.php**, only it will return all of its results as XML data. This data will be handled by the JavaScript in the Web browser. Start a new PHP script in your text editor or IDE.

1 This PHP page will not be viewed in the Web browser, so it begins with the opening PHP tag, not any HTML. (See **extra bits** on page 125.)

2 The **header()** function is used to send meta-information (i.e., not actual data). Here the **header()** function sends a Content-Type of text/xml. In layman's terms, this is a way of saying that XML data should be expected to follow.

```php
<?php # search_results_xml.php
header("Content-Type: text/xml");
echo '<?xml version="1.0" encoding="utf-8"
standalone="yes" ?>
<employees>
';
```

3 XML data begins wth the **declaration**.

4 All XML documents have **one root element**. This can be a made-up value, like **employees** here.

query the database

1 We make sure that **some value** was submitted for the **last name** or else there's no need to query the database.

2 The **MySQL connection script** is included.

```
...
<employees>
';
if (!empty($_GET['last_name'])) {
   require_once('mysql.inc.php');
   $q = "SELECT CONCAT(last_name, ', ', first_name),
email, department FROM employees LEFT JOIN departments
USING (department_id) WHERE last_name LIKE '" .
mysql_real_escape_string($_GET['last_name']) . "%'
ORDER BY last_name, first_name";
   $r = mysql_query($q, $dbc);
```

3 The query will return every employee's **name**, **email**, **address**, and **department** whose last name begins with the submitted letters. (See **extra bits** on page 125.)

4 The **mysql_real_escape_string()** function makes it safe to use the submitted value in a query.

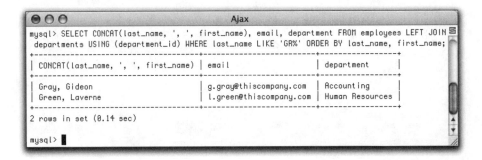

```
⬤⬤⬤                          Ajax
mysql> SELECT CONCAT(last_name, ', ', first_name), email, department FROM employees LEFT JOIN
  departments USING (department_id) WHERE last_name LIKE 'GR%' ORDER BY last_name, first_name;
+----------------------------------+----------------------------+------------------+
| CONCAT(last_name, ', ', first_name) | email                    | department       |
+----------------------------------+----------------------------+------------------+
| Gray, Gideon                     | g.gray@thiscompany.com     | Accounting       |
| Green, Laverne                   | l.green@thiscompany.com    | Human Resources  |
+----------------------------------+----------------------------+------------------+
2 rows in set (0.14 sec)

mysql> █
```

fetch the results

1 Check that **at least one record** was returned.

2 **Fetch all the records** and print them out as XML data.

```
...
$r = mysql_query($q, $dbc);
if (mysql_num_rows($r) > 0) {
  while ($row = mysql_fetch_array($r, MYSQL_NUM)) {
    echo "<employee>
<name>$row[0]</name>
<department>$row[2]</department>
<email>$row[1]</email>
</employee>\n";
  } // End of WHILE loop.
} // End of IF.
```

3 The **newline character** (\n) makes sure that whatever is printed next will go on the following line (like hitting Enter or Return on your keyboard).

```
<employees>
  - <employee>
      <name>Gray, Gideon</name>
      <department>Accounting</department>
      <email>g.gray@thiscompany.com</email>
  </employee>
  - <employee>
      <name>Green, Laverne</name>
      <department>Human Resources</department>
      <email>l.green@thiscompany.com</email>
  </employee>
</employees>
```

enabling an Ajax search

109

complete the PHP

1 **Close the database connection** (not required, but good form).

```
...
  } // End of IF.
  mysql_close($dbc);
} // End of $_GET['last_name'] IF.
// Complete the XML document.
echo '</employees>';
?>
```

2 **Close the root XML element** to complete the XML output. No need to use closing HTML tags!

3 Save this file as **search_ results_xml.php** and place it in (you guessed it) the same directory as everything else.

handle the response

The PHP page sends back XML data, which must be handled by the JavaScript. Add this new function to the **search.js** JavaScript file. (See **extra bits** on page 126.)

1 This JavaScript function is called when the **ajax** object's **readyState** value changes (see the **init()** function). The function receives the **ajax** object when called.

```
function handleResponse(ajax) {
  if (ajax.readyState == 4) {
    if ((ajax.status == 200) || (ajax.status == 304) )
  {
```

2 The function shouldn't do anything until **readyState** has a value of 4, meaning that the Ajax transaction is complete.

3 If the **status** code is equal to either 200 or 304, everything worked fine and we can use the returned results.

prepare the page

1 The **results** variable now refers to a specific area in the DOM of the HTML page.

```
...
if ((ajax.status == 200) || (ajax.status == 304) ) {
    var results = document.getElementById('results');
    results.style.display = 'block';
    while (results.hasChildNodes()) {
        results.removeChild(results.lastChild);
    }
```

2 The **results** area of the HTML page is initially invisible, so it needs to be made visible.

3 We remove every **node** that might exist within **results**. (See **extra bits** on page 126.)

handle the XML

1 The **data** variable now stores the PHP page's response as XML data. (See **extra bits** on page 126.)

2 The **names** variable is now an array of every element in the XML data with a tag name of **name**. If four names were returned, then **names** would now have four elements in it.

```
...
   results.removeChild(results.lastChild);
}
var data = ajax.responseXML;
var names = data.getElementsByTagName('name');
var departments = data.getElementsByTagName('departmen
t');
var emails = data.getElementsByTagName('email');
```

3 The **departments** variable is now an array of every element in the XML result with a tag name of **department**. Because of the way the PHP script generates the XML data, there should be one department for each name.

4 The **emails** variable is now an array of every element in the XML result with a tag name of **email**. Again, there'll be one email address for each name.

display the results

The results should be displayed like they are in the non-Ajax version. This is the generated HTML from that page, which should be replicated. (See **extra bits** on page 127.)

```
<p><span class="name">Gray, Gideon</span><br />
    <strong>Department</strong>: Accounting<br />
    <a href="mailto:g.gray@thiscompany.com">g.gray@thiscompany.com</a>
    </p>
<p><span class="name">Green, Laverne</span><br />
    <strong>Department</strong>: Human Resources<br />
    <a href="mailto:l.green@thiscompany.com">l.green@thiscompany.com</a>
    </p>
```

1 Before attempting to print the employees, we should confirm that some were returned by the PHP page. If at least one employee was returned in the XML data, then names will have more than 0 elements in it. You can count the number of elements in an array by referring to its length.

2 We'll need a slew of variables to add the values to the DOM.

```
...
var emails = data.getElementsByTagName('email');
if (names.length > 0) {
   var employee, span, name_node, dept_node, dept_label, br, strong, a, email;
```

3 The for loop will access every item in the *names* array. It counts from 0 (the first item in an array is at 0) to one less than the number of items in the array. With each iteration of the loop, the counter, `i`, is incremented.

```
for (var i = 0; i < names.length; i++) {
    employee = document.createElement('p');
```

4 Each employee returned by the PHP page will be put within an HTML paragraph (see the HTML source code on the previous page). So, within the loop, the first step is to create a new element of type p. This step adds a paragraph to the DOM, although the paragraph doesn't yet have anything in it, nor has it been placed on the page.

handle the name

The employee's name should be put within a **span** whose **class attribute** is **name**. This should be followed by a **break**.

```
<span class="name">Actual Name</span><br />
```

1 Another element, of type span, is created. (See **extra bits** on page 127.)

2 The **class attribute** of the span is given a value of **name**. So the text put within the span (see the next two steps) will be formatted as a **name**.

3 A different kind of node, a **text node**, is created. The value of the text node (which is to say the actual text) will be the value of the name returned in the XML data.

4 The text node is made a **child** of the span node. Therefore, the text node (which is the employee's name) is within the span.

```
...
employee = document.createElement('p');
span = document.createElement('span');
span.setAttribute('class', 'name');
name_node = document.createTextNode(names[i].
firstChild.nodeValue);
span.appendChild(name_node);
employee.appendChild(span);
br = document.createElement('br');
employee.appendChild(br);
```

5 The span is attached to the paragraph, created as **employee**.

6 A **break** element is added to the paragraph so that the pieces to follow will begin on the next line.

handle the department

The department has a little more formatting. It starts with the word **Department** with **strong** emphasis, followed by a colon and the actual department. There's another break at the end.

```
<strong>Department</strong>: Department Name<br />
```

1 Another element, of type **strong**, is created.

2 A text node with the value **Department** is created.

```
...
employee.appendChild(br);
strong = document.createElement('strong');
dept_label = document.createTextNode('Department');
strong.appendChild(dept_label);
employee.appendChild(strong);
```

3 The text node is made a child of the **strong** node. This places the text **Department** between the strong tags.

handle the department (cont)

4 Another text node is generated, with a value of the **colon**, followed by a **space**, followed by the **name of the department** from the XML data.

5 This latest text node is attached to the paragraph, which is **employee**.

```
dept_node = document.createTextNode(': ' +
departments[i].firstChild.nodeValue);
employee.appendChild(dept_node);
br = document.createElement('br');
employee.appendChild(br);
```

6 A **break** element is added to the paragraph so that the pieces to follow will begin on the next line.

handle the email

The email address is tricky because it should be linked so that clicking on the email address creates an email to that person.

```
<a href="mailto:address@example.com">address@example.
com</a>
```

1 Another element, of type *a*, is created. This type of element is for any link.

2 The **href attribute** of the *a* element is given a value of **mailto:** plus the person's email address from the XML data.

```
...
   employee.appendChild(br);
   a = document.createElement('a');
   a.setAttribute('href', 'mailto:' + emails[i].
firstChild.nodeValue);
```

handle the email (cont.)

3 A text node is created with a value of the employee's email address from the XML data.

4 The text node is made a **child** of the **a** node. Therefore, the text node (which is the employee's email address) is within the **a**.

```
email = document.
createTextNode(emails[i].firstChild.nodeValue);
    a.appendChild(email);
    employee.appendChild(a);
    results.appendChild(employee);
} // End of FOR loop.
```

5 The **a** element is attached to the paragraph.

6 The entire paragraph, which represents all of the employee's data, is made a child of the **results DIV**. (See **extra bits** on page 128.)

display no results

If the PHP page returned no results, a message should be displayed saying as much.

> **No employees were a match.**

1 A new element of type **p** is created.

2 The **class attribute** of the paragraph is given a value of **error**.

```
...
  } // End of FOR loop.
} else { // No employees, print a message.
  var node1 = document.createElement('p');
  node1.setAttribute('class', 'error');
  var node2 = document.createTextNode('No employees
were a match.');
  node1.appendChild(node2);
  results.appendChild(node1);
}
```

3 A text node is created with a value of
No employees were a match.

4 The text node is made a **child** of the paragraph node.

5 The paragraph is made a child of the **results DIV**, thereby putting the paragraph onto the page.

complete the function

If we didn't get a valid status code back from the Ajax request, we should formally submit the form to the handling PHP page (as if the Ajax layer didn't exist at all).

```
...
            results.appendChild(node1);
        }
    } else { // Bad status code, submit the form.
        document.getElementById('search_form').submit();
    }
  } // End of readyState IF.
} // End of handleResponse() function.
```

enabling an Ajax search

test the Ajax layer

1 **Load the HTML page** in your Web browser.

The address **must begin with** http:// for this to work.

2 Enter a letter or two and click **GO**.

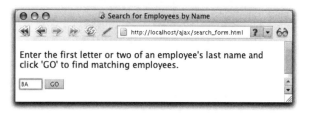

3 The HTML page should show the results without reloading the page or going to a new page.

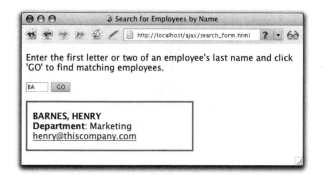

4 Enter invalid letters and click **GO** to see the result if no employees in the database matched the search term.

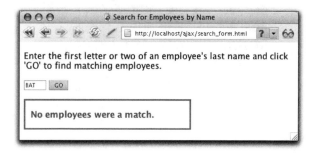

extra bits

what we'll do p. 100

- In this example, I suggest that users enter only a couple of letters because the database has only 20 records in it. With the employees entered in chapter 1, "creating the database," **Gr** will return two records but **Gre** only one. If your database had more names in it, entering longer values would be appropriate.

add the Ajax elements p. 102

- The **ajax.js** file, written in chapter 3, "browsing using Ajax," defines a function that returns a **browser-specific XMLHttpRequest object**. This file is needed by any page that performs any Ajax operations.

- Because the **DIV**, where the results will be reported, has an **id value of results**, it'll be formatted according to the rules dictated in **style. css**. This is the same as the **results DIV in dept_form. html and in add_employee. html**. For starters, the **DIV** will be invisible when the page is first viewed.

apply the Ajax layer p. 103

- Most of this code is exactly like that in **dept.js and add_ employee.js**. The big difference at first is the name of the form being referenced. It's in the rest of the code—what should be done when the form is submitted—that the big differences can be found.

set up the Ajax p. 105

- The **encodeURIComponent()** function makes it safe to pass in the URL whatever value the user entered in the form.

- By passing the form data in the URL, we ensure that the Ajax request will be made to **search_results_xml. php?last_name=XXX**, where **XXX** represents what the user typed in the text box.

prepare for XML p. 107

- The PHP script sends its response as XML data, not as a normal Web page. Everything PHP will print will be part of this XML and there will be no HTML output.

- The XML data being created is really like the data in an HTML page, where there's one root element and any number of nested subelements. For this example, the root element will be called **employees** and there will be zero or more subelements called **employee**.

- If the PHP page does not use the `header()` function to set the `Content-Type`, the JavaScript that receives this response will not recognize it as XML.

query the database p. 108

- To debug any PHP-MySQL problems, you'll need to **print out the query** to inspect its syntax. You should also invoke the `mysql_error()` function to see what problems the database reports.

- A useful debugging technique when working with XML data is to verify that your PHP script is returning valid XML. To see the result of the PHP page, either use JavaScript to access `ajax.responseText` (in the `handleResponse()` function) or submit your form to the PHP page directly (without using JavaScript).

- For directly viewing XML in your Web browser, you'll want to use a browser that supports the format. At the time of this writing, this includes recent versions of Internet Explorer and Firefox, but not Safari.

extra bits (cont.)

handle the response p. 111

- In the **init()** function, we tell the JavaScript to call a function called **handleResponse()** whenever the **readyState** value changes. This value will change multiple times during an Ajax request, so this function will be called multiple times.

- The XMLHttpRequest **status** attribute stores the **HTTP status code** returned by the server-side page. There are dozens of status codes from **200**, meaning that everything was OK, to values over 500, which are normally server errors. A status code of **304** indicates that the page was found but had not been modified since a certain date and time.

prepare the page p. 112

- The new trick in this specific example is the use of **nodes** as the way of manipulating the page's content. If you think of the Document Object Model as a tree, then a node is a branch on that tree; each

branch has a parent (which is either another branch or the tree trunk) and some have children (more branches). To place content on the page, we'll add branches to the **results** section. So to prepare the page for the XML data, we need to clear out any existing nodes in **results**. We do so by applying the **removeChild()** function to **results**, removing the last node, until there are no more nodes left.

handle the XML p. 113

- The server's response is available in two attributes of the XMLHttpRequest object. It can be found as plain text in **responseText** or as XML data in **responseXML**.

- The XML data can be accessed just like elements on an HTML page, using the Document Object Model. So **data.getElementsByTagName ('name')** refers to every item in the XML data with a name of **name**.

display the results p. 114

- This example, which uses both nodes in the DOM and XML data from PHP, is the most complicated in the book. The idea is simple, though: take the HTML code generated by the non-Ajax PHP script and duplicate it using Ajax. So everything in the last half of this chapter is just a matter of using nodes, the DOM, and XML to that end.

- So many JavaScript variables are declared because creating nodes in the DOM is a multi-step process, as you'll see in this chapter. And since each employee's record has multiple elements—one **paragraph**, one span, two **breaks**, one *a* link, one **strong**, plus three pieces of text (the name, the department, and the email address)—it'll be easiest to follow using many different variables.

- The syntax of the **for** loop is a common way to access every item found in an array. Within the loop, the specific array item is accessed via `arrayname[i]`.

- The **createElement()** function is the most important for adding nodes to the DOM. It makes the element, but you then have to add it to the page using **appendChild()**.

handle the name p. 116

- The **setAttribute()** function takes two arguments: the name of the attribute to set and the value it should be given.

- To get the values from the XML data, refer to `arrayname[i].firstChild.nodeValue`. The `arrayname[i]` refers to a specific element in the array; `firstChild` refers to the first branch of that element (which we know is the only node each element has); and **nodeValue** refers to the actual content found there (which is the text).

- The **appendChild()** function adds the element in parentheses to the element named before the period.

extra bits (cont.)

handle the email p. 120

- It isn't until the **employee** element, with all its subelements (or nodes), is appended to the **results DIV** that the employee data will appear on the HTML page.

- If the PHP script returns five employee records, then the **results DIV** will end up having five child nodes. Each of these nodes will be a paragraph element, within which are the **span** for the name, the **strong** element and other department text, the **a** element for the email address, and the two breaks.

appendix
where to go from here

This book provides all the code and knowledge required to add Ajax functionality to a Web site. But, as with most things, there's a lot more to be learned. This appendix will steer you in other useful directions and provide the occasional code snippet as alternatives to the code used elsewhere in the book.

Ajax issues

Ajax is a wonderful technology that can greatly enhance a user's Web experience, but it's not perfect. In particular, you should be aware of the following limitations:

1 If a user's browser does not **support JavaScript**, Ajax is useless. (See **extra bits** on page 146.)

2 The results of Ajax-enabled pages **cannot be bookmarked** without taking extra steps.

3 The user **cannot use the back button or** their browser's **history** to review previous results (again without taking extra steps).

4 **Search engines** cannot index Ajax pages.

5 Ajax applications can be more **demanding of the browser**.

6 Because Ajax pages change the standard client-server relationship, their use may be **confusing for the end user**.

7 Ajax requires that the user **be online** the entire time.

Ajax alternatives

It may seem strange to discuss other options in a book about Ajax, but you can get a better understanding of a thing by knowing what the alternatives are. What can be accomplished via Ajax may also be possible using:

1 **iFrames**: While not as powerful as Ajax, iFrames are well supported by most browsers. iFrames often still make use of JavaScript; therefore, they can have some of the same issues as Ajax.

2 **Flash**: This is an extremely useful technology but requires that the user install the Flash plug-in for their browser.

3 **Java applets**: Like Flash, Java applets have a wide range of uses and abilities but require installed browser support.

introducing JSON

JSON (JavaScript Simple Object Notation) provides an alternative to XML for transmittng data. Here is some sample XML data from Chapter 7, "enabling an Ajax search":

```
<employees>
    <employee>
<name>Gray, Gideon</name>
<department>Accounting</department>
<email>g.gray@thiscompany.com</email>
</employee>
    <employee>
<name>Green, Laverne</name>
<department>Human Resources</department>
<email>l.green@thiscompany.com</email>
</employee>
</employees>
```

Here's how that same data would look in JSON format (actually, all the data would be on one line, without spaces, but I've spaced it out for clarity):

```
[
{"name":"Gray, Gideon","department":"Accounting","emai
l":"g.gray@thiscompany.com"},
{"name":"Green, Laverne","department":"Human
Resources","email":"l.green@thiscompany.com"}
]
```

Because **JSON data is JavaScript**, it's arguably easier to work with than XML. And the same data will likely be smaller in JSON than in XML (meaning a smaller transfer size from the server to the client). See **extra bits** on page 146 for why you shouldn't use JSON.

sending JSON

Here's how the **search_results_xml.php** script from Chapter 7 would be rewritten to send JSON data instead of XML:

```php
<?php # search_results_json.php
header("Content-type: application/json");
if (!empty($_GET['last_name'])) {
  require_once('mysql.inc.php');
  $q = "SELECT CONCAT(last_name, ', ', first_name),
email, department FROM employees LEFT JOIN departments
USING (department_id) WHERE last_name LIKE '" . mysql_
real_escape_string($_GET['last_name']) . "%' ORDER BY
last_name, first_name";
  $r = mysql_query($q, $dbc);
  if (mysql_num_rows($r) > 0) {
```

1 The **content-type** header indicates what type of data is being sent by this script.

2 **Initialize an array** that will store the results.

```php
$data = array();
while ($row = mysql_fetch_array($r, MYSQL_NUM)) {
    $data[] = array ('name' => $row[0],
    'department' => $row[2],
    'email' => $row[1]);
    } // End of WHILE loop.
    echo json_encode($data) . "\n";
}
mysql_close($dbc);
} // End of $_GET['last_name'] IF.
?>
```

3 Add each record as a new item in the **$data** array.

4 Use a **library** to turn the array into JSON format, and print the results. (See **extra bits** on page 146.)

accessing JSON data

To finish changing the search from Chapter 7 to use JSON, you must alter the **search.js** file. All of the relevant changes go within the **handleResponse()** function (although you also have to change the reference to the **search_results_xml.php** script earlier in the JavaScript file, if you rename that file):

1 Retrieve the data in **ajax.responseText**.

2 Convert the data to an object using **eval()**.

```
...
while (results.hasChildNodes()) {
results.removeChild(results.lastChild);
}
var data = eval('(' + ajax.responseText + ')');
if (data.length > 0) {
...
```

3 Check that **some records** were returned by looking at the array's size.

using JSON data

To update the DOM using the JSON data, complete the modification of the **handleResponse()** function:

1 Access every returned record using a **loop**.

```
...
if (data.length > 0) {
  var employee, span, name_node, dept_node, dept_
label, br, strong, a, email;
  for (var i = 0; i < data.length; i++) {
    employee = document.createElement('p');
    span = document.createElement('span');
    span.setAttribute('class', 'name');
```

using JSON data (cont.)

2 Access the individual elements using **dot syntax**.

```
name_node = document.createTextNode(data[i].name);
span.appendChild(name_node);
employee.appendChild(span);
br = document.createElement('br');
employee.appendChild(br);
strong = document.createElement('strong');
dept_label = document.createTextNode('Department')
;
strong.appendChild(dept_label);
employee.appendChild(strong);
dept_node = document.createTextNode(': ' +
data[i].department);
employee.appendChild(dept_node);
br = document.createElement('br');
employee.appendChild(br);
a = document.createElement('a');
a.setAttribute('href', 'mailto:' + data[i].email);
email = document.createTextNode(data[i].email);
a.appendChild(email);
employee.appendChild(a);
results.appendChild(employee);
  } // End of FOR loop.
} else { // No employees, print a message.
...
```

web resources

Along with the frameworks sites listed on the following pages, you might find these Ajax-specific sites worth your time (I've whittled the hundreds and hundreds of Ajax sites down to a good starting handful):

1 Ajax Patterns (**www.ajaxpatterns.org**) has tons of Ajax resources (in programming, a **pattern** is a best practice for solving problems).

2 AJAX Matters (**www.ajaxmatters.com**) has a lot of articles on various Ajax-related subjects.

3 Ajaxian (**www.ajaxian.com**) has been around since the beginning of Ajax and has articles covering a range of Ajax-based topics.

4 Douglas Crockford's Wrrrld Wide Web (**www.crockford.com**) is short on frills but long on usefulness. Crockford is a prominent JavaScript developer and one of the people behind JSON.

5 You can find the first coining of the word Ajax at **http://adaptivepath.com/publications/essays/archives/000385.php**.

JavaScript frameworks

A **framework** is an **established library of code** that can be used to more easily do the things you'd otherwise program by hand (as I do in this book). Here are a handful of the dozens and dozens of frameworks available. (See **extra bits** on page 147.)

Name	URL
Prototype	`www.prototypejs.org`
Rico	`www.openrico.org`
Dojo Toolkit	`www.dojotoolkit.org`
jQuery	`http://jquery.com`
Sarissa	`http://dev.abiss.gr/sarissa/`
script.aculo.us	`http://script.aculo.us`
mootools	`www.mootools.net`
Yahoo! User Interface Library	`http://developer.yahoo.com/yui/`
Spry	`http://labs.adobe.com/technologies/spry/`

PHP-Ajax frameworks

Instead of using a JavaScript-specific framework, you could use one that helps with both the JavaScript and the PHP. The two most popular are:

1 SAJAX (Simple Ajax Toolkit): **www.modernmethod.com/sajax/**

2 xajax: **www.xajaxproject.org**

3 PEAR::HTML_AJAX: **http://pear.php.net/package/.HTML_AJAX**

debugging JavaScript

Mastering the art of debugging is crucial when using any programming language, and Ajax/JavaScript is no exception. I could write an entire book, or at least a full chapter, on the subject, but you'll find this short list of the best tools and techniques helpful:

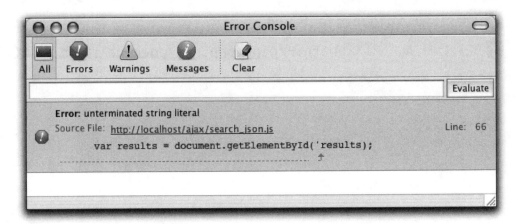

1 A **JavaScript console**: Firefox has a JavaScript console built in. It'll print errors and other necessary messages to aid your debugging. If an Ajax page doesn't work as expected, this is the first place you should look.

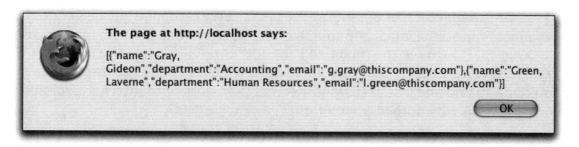

The page at http://localhost says:

[{"name":"Gray, Gideon","department":"Accounting","email":"g.gray@thiscompany.com"},{"name":"Green, Laverne","department":"Human Resources","email":"l.green@thiscompany.com"}]

OK

2 **JavaScript alerts**: I recommend using alerts to confirm what functions are executed and what the values of variables are.

```
alert('Inside the handleResponse() function.');
alert(ajax.responseText);
```

debugging JavaScript (cont.)

3 A **DOM inspector**: Because most Ajax applications change a page's content dynamically, just looking at the source of the page won't be of use. Instead, use a DOM inspector to see the modified page content. Firefox has one built in (on Windows, you'll need to do a custom install of Firefox to add the inspector). You can also find and install DOM inspectors that work with Internet Explorer and Safari, but why bother when Firefox's already exists?

4 The **Venkman JavaScript Debugger** (www.mozilla.org/projects/venkman): This is a sophisticated JavaScript debugger that can be used through Firefox.

5 JSLint (www.jslint.com): This program performs basic syntax checks on JavaScript. Just paste your JavaScript in the box on the JSLint Web site and click the JSLint button.

6 Firebug (www.getfirebug.com): This FireFox extension provides a wealth of debugging tools, covering HTML, CSS, JavaScript, and the DOM.

7 **Firefox Firefox Firefox**: In case it's not clear from this list (where Firefox is singled out four times), Firefox is clearly the best browser for debugging Ajax applications (it may be the best browser period). You'll need to test your Ajax scripts on other browsers to verify support, but when it comes to debugging, use Firefox first!

extra bits

Ajax issues p. 130

- With the code in this book, every example will work whether or not the user's browser supports Ajax. The examples were purposefully designed this way, so that if the nice Ajax layer won't work, the user isn't left behind. This is an approach you should maintain as much as possible.

- Ajax pages cannot be bookmarked, recorded in the browser's history, or listed in search engines because the changes aren't reflected in a URL. By taking some extra steps, it's possible to overcome some of these limitations. Search the Web for techniques.

- It's important to give obvious clues to the user when something is happening or has happened. In this book, I use an overt formatting of Ajax results to make the changes apparent.

introducing JSON p. 132–133

- The biggest concern with using JSON is that there are some **security risks** involved. The **eval()** function actually runs the received text as JavaScript code, meaning that the Ajax process could be hacked if the data could be manipulated. Search the Web for more on this subject and for possible safeguards.

- Another issue with JSON is that the syntax is **very, very particular**, much more so than XML. Using a library to create the JSON data will give more reliable results.

sending JSON p. 134–135

- Instead of trying to create the exact JSON syntax programmatically, I think it's best to use an external library that will do this for you. In this script, I'm making use of the **PECL JSON** class (which must be installed; see **http://pecl.php.net**—it's **enabled by default as of PHP 5.2**).

- Alternatively, see the official JSON Web site (**www.json.org**) for includable PHP libraries that can perform the conversion of an array to JSON.

JavaScript frameworks p. 140

- There are three main downsides to using frameworks. The first is that they require **some effort to learn** how to use them. The second is that they normally greatly **increase the amount of data** that a user must download from your site (which is to say, frameworks are almost inherently bloated). Finally, you must pay attention to new releases of a framework, as they might **patch security holes**.

- In choosing a framework, factor in **how many and what browsers it supports, how large it is** (in terms of file size that the user will end up downloading), and **how well documentated** it is.

index

index

F

index

form data
   preparing, 65–66, 83
   validating, 50–52, 57, 68–71, 84
forms. **see also** HTML pages
   elements, adding, 47–48, 57
form's action values, 14
frameworks
   JavaScript, 140, 147
   PHP-Ajax, 141
functions
   calling, 35–36, 40
   making, 27–28, 39

G

GET method
   when adding records, 57, 82, 83
   when browsing, 22
   when searching, 91, 97,
   105getXMLHttp
    RequestObject( ) function
   when adding records, 63
   when browsing, 27, 28, 29, 39
   when searching, 103

H

handleResponse( ) function
   JSON and, 136, 137
    when adding records, 64, 79, 84
    when searching, 105, 111, 125
header( ) function
   preparing for XML and, 67, 84
   when searching, 107, 125
href attribute, 119

HTML
   generated when searching,
   114–115
   relationship to Ajax, xi
HTML, XHTML, and CSS, Sixth
Edition: Visual QuickStart
Guide, xviii, 24
HTML pages. **see also** testing
   creating, 22, 24
   creating, when adding records,
   45–48
   creating, when browsing, 12, 13–
   14, 22
   creating, when searching, 88, 89–
   91, 97
   modifying when adding records,
   62, 82
   modifying when browsing, 37
   modifying when searching, 102
   style sheets and, 20
   testing, when adding records, 54–
   56, 80–81
   testing, when browsing, 21, 24, 38
   testing, when searching, 96, 123
HTTP status code, 126

I

IDE (integrated development
   environment), xiv
iFrames, 131
indexing Ajax pages, 130
init( ) function
   adding records and, 63, 75, 85
   when searching, 126

index

SQL
   creating tables and, 6, 8
   downloading commands, 9, 10
strip_tags( ) function, 57
strong node, 117
style sheets, CSS
   creating, 12, 19–20, 24
   page appearance and, 45, 89
   using, 20

T

tables
   creating, 5–6, 9
   populating, 7–8, 10
testing
   when adding, 54–56, 80–81
   when browsing, 21, 24, 38
   when searching, 96, 123
text editors
   HTML pages and, 22
   necessity for, xiv
text nodes, 116, 120
< title > values, 13

U

user names, PHP scripts and, 23

V

validating form data, 50–52, 57,
   68–70, 84
values
   < title > values, 13
   adding numeric values to forms, 52
Venkman JavaScript Debugger, 145

W

Web browsers
   Ajax basics and, x, 13
examples in this book and, xiv
   testing Ajax and, 42
   using phpMyAdmin and, 2
   XML support and, 84, 125
   XMLHttpRequest object and, 28
Web resources
   companion site to this book, xvii
   for further information, 139
   JSON Web site, 146
   PECL JSON class, 146
   PHP libraries, 146
What You See Is What You Get
   (WYSIWYG), xiv

X

XML
   completing when adding records,
      73–74, 84
   debugging, 84, 125
   Firefox and, 84, 125
handling when adding records, 77
   handling when searching, 113
   header( ) function and, 67, 84
   JSON as alternative to, 132–138
   preparing for when adding records,
      67, 83
   preparing for when searching, 107
XMLHttpRequest object
   browser-specific, 82
   importance of in Ajax, xi
   when adding records, 44
   when searching, 103, 124